Instructional Strategies for Effective Teaching

Xianxuan
James H.
STRONGE
XU

Solution Tree | Press

a division of

Solution Tree

555 North Morton Street
Bloomington, IN 47404
800.733.6786 (toll free) / 812.336.7700
FAX: 812.336.7790

email: info@solution-tree.com
solution-tree.com

Visit **go.solution-tree.com/instruction** to download the reproducibles in this book.

Printed in the United States of America

19 18 17   2 3 4 5

Library of Congress Cataloging-in-Publication Data

Stronge, James H.

Instructional strategies for effective teaching / by James H. Stronge and Xianxuan Xu.

    pages cm

Includes bibliographical references and index.

ISBN 978-1-936763-75-7 (perfect bound) 1. Effective teaching I. Xu, Xianxuan. II. Title.

LB1025.3.S7888 2016

371.102--dc23

                2015026231

Solution Tree

Jeffrey C. Jones, CEO
Edmund M. Ackerman, President

Solution Tree Press

President: Douglas M. Rife
Senior Acquisitions Editor: Amy Rubenstein
Editorial Director: Lesley Bolton
Art Director: Rian Anderson
Managing Production Editor: Caroline Weiss
Production Editor: Rachel Rosolina
Copy Editor: Miranda Addonizio
Proofreader: Elisabeth Abrams
Text and Cover Designer: Rachel Smith

Acknowledgments

Solution Tree Press would like to thank the following reviewers:

Melissa Jordan
Science Teacher
Sarah Scott Middle School
Terre Haute, Indiana

Charles Maranzano Jr.
Superintendent
Vernon Township School District
Vernon, New Jersey

Debbie Schuler
Administrator of Instructional Services
Florida School for the Deaf and the Blind
St. Augustine, Florida

Table of Contents

Reproducible pages are in italics.

About the Authors

James H. Stronge, PhD, is president of Stronge and Associates Educational Consulting, an educational consulting company that focuses on teacher and leader effectiveness with projects internationally and in many U.S. states. Additionally, he is the Heritage Professor of Education, a distinguished professorship in the Educational Policy, Planning, and Leadership program at the College of William and Mary, in Williamsburg, Virginia.

Dr. Stronge's research interests include policy and practice related to teacher effectiveness, teacher and administrator evaluation, and teacher selection. He has worked with state departments of education, school districts, and U.S. and international education organizations to design and implement evaluation and hiring systems for teachers, administrators, and support personnel. Recently, he completed work on new teacher and principal evaluation systems for American international schools in conjunction with the Association of American Schools in South America and supported by the U.S. Department of State. Dr. Stronge has made more than 350 presentations at regional, national, and international conferences and has conducted workshops for educational organizations extensively throughout the United States and internationally. Among his current research projects are international comparative studies of national award-winning teachers in the United States and China and influences of economic and societal trends on student academic performance in countries globally.

Dr. Stronge has authored, coauthored, or edited twenty-six books and approximately two hundred articles, chapters, and technical reports. His 1994 book, *Educating Homeless Children and Adolescents: Evaluating Policy and Practice* received the Outstanding Academic Book Award from the American Library Association.

Dr. Stronge was a founding member of the board of directors for the Consortium for Research on Educational Accountability and Teacher Evaluation (CREATE). In 2011, he was honored with the Frank E. Flora Lamp of Knowledge Award, presented by the Virginia Association of Secondary School Principals for "bringing honor to the profession" and his "record of outstanding contributions." He was selected as the 2012 national recipient of the Millman Award from CREATE in recognition of his work in the field of teacher and administrator evaluation.

Xianxuan Xu, PhD, is a senior research associate at Stronge and Associates Educational Consulting. Dr. Xu received her doctorate from the College of William and Mary's Educational Policy, Planning, and Leadership program. Her research interests are teacher effectiveness, professional development, and teacher and principal evaluation. She is also particularly interested in researching the relationship between culture and educational issues such as teaching, learning, and leadership. She has presented research findings at various U.S. conferences, including the American Educational Research Association, University Council for Educational Administration, and National Evaluation Institute. She is also a contributing author to *Principal Evaluation: Standards, Rubrics, and Tools for Effective Performance* and *West Meets East: Best Practices From Expert Teachers in the U.S. and China*.

Visit www.strongeandassociates.com to learn more about Dr. Stronge and Dr. Xu's work.

To book James H. Stronge or Xianxuan Xu for professional development, contact pd@solution-tree.com.

Introduction

When teachers improve, students improve. John Hattie (2012) summarizes this point well, saying, "Teachers are among the most powerful influences in learning" (p. 22). A logical reaction to this point is to wonder how teachers exert this influence on student learning. Moreover, how do they support and sustain teacher growth school by school and year by year? This book focuses on the important practices of effective teachers, specifically instructional delivery.

To illuminate what occurs in highly effective teachers' classrooms, we conducted a multiyear research study in which we examined the instructional practices and beliefs of national award-winning teachers in the United States and China (Grant et al., 2014). The findings from the study reveal that exceptional teachers in both countries:

- Consistently use a wide variety of instructional activities (in fact, about nine instructional activities per lesson, on average)

- Engage students to a high degree

- Focus on varying cognitive levels during instruction

Based on our study, we know that the number, types, and selection of instructional methods along with the connectivity among those methods are important to effective teaching.

Instructional Methods

Portions of this material appear in Stronge, Grant, and Xu (2015).

Hattie (2012) reports that what teachers do and how they teach, collectively, yield an effect size (ES) of 0.62—quite a high impact on student achievement. Specific instructional strategies independently produce a dramatic improvement on student learning as well—consider microteaching (0.88), metacognitive strategies (0.69), and direct instruction (0.59). In essence, instructional methods matter (Hattie, 2012).

One prominent instructional method, questioning, can be a highly effective tool when used properly, as it has an effect size of 0.46 (Guo, Tsai, Chang, & Huang, 2007; Hattie, 2012). Questioning not only provides students with an opportunity to think critically and become more informed about their learning but also yields important input for teachers to support instructional modifications (Stronge, 2007). Effective teachers and ineffective teachers use questioning in substantially different ways. Effective teachers ask both lower-order and higher-order questions to improve the comprehension of students of all learning abilities. In addition, the questions they ask are relevant to the intended learning outcomes and serve to facilitate learning activities. Ineffective teachers, on the other hand, ask about 93 percent of all the questions, according to a study of science classrooms (Reinsvold & Cochran, 2012). The study also finds that these teachers tend to provide little wait time, ask questions at the lowest cognitive level, and use closed-ended questions. Another case study finds that effective teachers ask higher-level questions approximately seven times more often than teachers considered ineffective (Stronge, Ward, Tucker, & Hindman, 2007).

There is no single classroom practice that is effective with all subject matter and all grade levels in all circumstances. And effective teachers recognize that no single instructional strategy can be used in all situations. Rather, they develop and call on a broad repertoire of approaches that have proven successful for them. Effective instruction involves a dynamic interplay among content to be learned, pedagogical methods applied, characteristics of individual learners, and the context in which the learning is to occur (Schalock, Schalock, Cowart, & Myton, 1993). Ultimately, subject matter knowledge, pedagogical skills, and an inspiration for instructional innovation and development can liberate individual teachers to explore the diversification and richness of daily practice.

An Overview of the Book

Based on a review of research on instructional delivery methods, *Instructional Strategies for Effective Teaching* is organized around ten key instructional methods.

1. Classroom discussion
2. Concept attainment
3. Concept mapping
4. Cooperative learning
5. Direct instruction
6. Mastery learning
7. Memorization and mnemonic instruction
8. Inquiry-based learning
9. Self-regulated learning
10. Meaningful feedback

Note that these are not the only methods that one can or should consider; rather, from the dozens available, we've selected ten methods that are well researched in terms of their impact on student learning and that effective teachers frequently use.

We present each of these ten instructional methods in its own chapter along with explicit strategies teachers can employ in the everyday life of an effective classroom. To make the featured methods relevant and useful, each chapter contains the following sections.

- An introduction to the instructional method
- What research says about the instructional method
- How to move from research to practice

To end each chapter, we include several handouts to help teachers use these instructional methods immediately. Our intent is for teachers and school leaders to take the methods they find useful right off of the page and put them into practice as seamlessly as possible.

Teachers can use many of the featured methods for self-assessment and reflection. They also help administrators assess instructional practices from the formative perspective. As table I.1 summarizes, we support three specific groups of educators in the important work of delivering effective teaching.

Table I.1: Goals for Each Audience

Audience	Goals of Book
Teachers improving practice	• Self-reflection • Guided study • Teacher-directed growth
Teachers teaching teachers	• Mentor tips • Instructional coaching tips • Peer networks
Leaders supporting teachers	• Directed growth • Supervisor support for teachers • Coordinated curriculum

Summary: So Where Do We Go From Here?

Instruction is a process in which teachers apply a range of instructional strategies to communicate and interact with students around academic content and to support student engagement. We know from both research and personal experience that teachers who have similar professional qualifications (such as degree, certification, or years of experience) teach differently in their classrooms and vary significantly in their performances when helping students learn academically. The primary difference between effective and ineffective teachers does not lie in the amount of knowledge they have about subject content, the type of certificate they hold, the highest degree they earned, or even the years they have been teaching. Rather, the difference lies more fundamentally in the manner in which they deliver their knowledge and the skills they use while interacting with their students.

Our goal for this book is to make the delivery of content and the interactions with students around the content more dynamic, engaging, and successful. It is our hope that this guide on instructional methods will motivate you to broaden your instructional versatility and creativity and that you find it practical, solidly researched, and easy to use. Now, let's put these methods to use in your school or classroom.

Chapter 1
Classroom Discussion

Classroom discussion is an instructional method that engages learners in a conversation for the purpose of learning content and related skills. By engaging in quality classroom discussion, students build understanding of the subject matter, delve deeper into their own perspectives, present their own views verbally, support their arguments with evidence, listen and respond critically, take notes, and critique themselves and others.

According to Michael Hale and Elizabeth City (2006), "student-centered discussions are conversations in which students wrestle with ideas and engage in open-ended questions together through dialogue" (p. 3). In particular, there are two goals for a quality classroom discussion (Hale & City, 2006).

1. Teachers must deepen students' understanding of ideas in instructional content, as well as their own ideas and the ideas of others.

2. Teachers must develop students' abilities to engage in a civil, intellectually challenging discussion of ideas.

Hale and City (2006) note that "through close examination and discussion of ideas, along with the use of texts and other learning materials, students develop the skills and habits of reading analytically, listening carefully, citing evidence, disagreeing respectfully, and being open-minded" (pp. 3–4). Similarly, Stephen Brookfield and Stephen Preskill (2005) write that discussion causes "people to expand their horizons, develop new interests, and appreciate new perspectives" (p. 34), as suggested in the following fifteen benefits of discussion (Brookfield & Preskill, 2005).

1. Helps students explore a diversity of perspectives

2. Increases students' awareness of and tolerance for ambiguity or complexity

3. Helps students recognize and investigate their assumptions

4. Encourages attentive, respectful listening

5. Develops new appreciation for continuing differences

6. Increases intellectual agility

7. Helps students connect with a topic

8. Shows respect for students' voices and experiences

9. Helps students learn the processes and habits of democratic discourse

10. Affirms students as cocreators of knowledge

11. Develops the capacity for the clear communication of ideas and meaning

12. Develops habits of collaborative learning

13. Increases breadth of understanding and makes students more empathic

14. Helps students develop skills of synthesis and integration

15. Leads to transformation

Virtually all teachers have experience organizing and leading classroom discussions; in fact, along with lecture and questioning, discussion is one of the most prominent instructional techniques used in classrooms—especially secondary classrooms. By looking at the research on classroom discussion, it's easy to see why.

What Research Says About Classroom Discussion

In an experimental study that examines the effect of collaborative classroom discussion on the quality of students' essay writing by randomly assigning students to two groups either with or without discussion, Alina Reznitskaya et al. (2001) find that students who participate in collaborative discussion use a significantly greater number of relevant arguments, counterarguments, rebuttals, formal argument devices, and text information than students who do not engage in discussion. Another experimental study by Clark Chinn, Angela O'Donnell, and Theresa Jinks (2000) finds that both content and structure of the discussion matter for collaborative discussion learning. By diagramming the discourse structures that emerge during small-group discussion in science classes, the authors characterize these structures as a network of arguments and counterarguments with varied degrees of complexity and depth. They also find that student content learning is associated with the quality of those argument structures: the more complex the discourse structures, the better the student learning.

Karen Murphy, Ian Wilkinson, Anna Soter, Maeghan Hennessey, and John Alexander (2009) reviewed empirical research to determine the effects of classroom discussion on students' comprehension and learning of text. Results reveal that discussion approaches produce substantial increases in the amount of student talk and reductions in teacher talk, as well as considerable improvement in text comprehension. However, there is no consistent evidence that discussion can increase students' inferential comprehension and critical thinking and reasoning, and the effects are mediated by factors such as the nature of the outcome measure. Table 1.1 presents the specific effect sizes of various discussion approaches on a number of student outcome measures.

What we conclude from the review of studies reported here is that discussion has an overall positive impact on advancing students' learning; however, the effectiveness of discussion is contingent on how the discussion is structured and how sensitive it is to the instructional goals. For instance, if the purpose is for general comprehension or comprehension of explicit meaning of texts, instructional conversation in which teachers and students respond to each other's provocative ideas and experiences would be a better option. If the learning goal is to enhance students' critical-thinking skills, then collaborative reasoning would be a more appropriate approach, as students would have to engage in reasoned argumentation.

How to Move From Research to Practice

Despite the ubiquitous nature of discussions, there are guidelines that effective teachers should consider as they seek to improve their skills as discussion designers and facilitators. Ronald Hyman (1980) proposes four major types of discussion for use in classrooms.

1. **Policy discussion:** This type of discussion focuses on students' reactions toward certain issues and requires the group to take a stand.

2. **Problem-solving discussion:** This type of discussion requires groups of learners to seek an answer to a problem or conflict.

3. **Explaining discussion:** This type of discussion asks students to analyze and articulate causes and effects.

4. **Predicting discussion:** This type of discussion prompts students to predict the probable consequences of a given situation or position.

Teachers determine which discussion approach to use based on the learning objectives. For instance, they can use a problem-solving discussion for more sophisticated learning processes and can include all the major components of problem identification, problem analysis, potential solutions, solution evaluation, decision making, and even solution implementation. On the other hand, discussion can be streamlined to involve only formulating hypotheses and predicting probable consequences.

Ways to Start a Discussion

There are many ways to start a classroom discussion. Murphy et al. (2009) review nine such approaches (the effect sizes of which can be seen in table 1.1).

First is *collaborative reasoning*. In this strategy,

> the teacher poses a central question deliberately chosen to evoke varying points of view. Students adopt a position on the issue and generate reasons that support their position. Using the text, as well as personal experiences and background knowledge, students proceed to evaluate reasons, to consider alternative points of view, and to challenge the arguments of others. (Murphy et al., 2009, p. 742)

Table 1.1: Effect Sizes of Discussion Approaches

	General Comprehension	Text-Explicit Comprehension	Text-Implicit Comprehension	Scriptally Implicit Comprehension	Critical Thinking and Reasoning	Argumentations	Metacognition
Critical-Analytic — Discussions that engage the learners' querying minds, prompt them to ask questions, and encourage more subjective, critical responses toward the text							
Collaborative Reasoning	0.262	0.490	0.082	0.668	2.465	0.260	0.284
Philosophy for Children	0.333	—	—	—	0.236	0.214	—
Paideia Seminar	—	—	—	0.428	—	—	—
Efferent — Discussions that prompt text-focused responses and give prominence to reading to acquire and retrieve particular information							
Questioning the Author	−0.205	0.899	—	0.627	2.499	—	—
Instructional Conversation	2.798	1.336	0.568	0.871	—	—	—
Junior Great Books	0.333	0.331	1.124	—	0.718	—	—
Expressive — Discussions that prompt a learner-centered response and give prominence to the learners' affective responses to the text or their spontaneous emotive connections to the text							
Literature Circles	0.426	—	2.136	—	—	—	—
Grand Conversation	—	—	0.822	—	—	—	—
Book Club	—	—	—	—	—	—	−1.073

Text-Explicit Comprehension: Comprehension requiring information that is explicitly stated, usually within a sentence

Text-Implicit Comprehension: Comprehension requiring integration of information across sentences, paragraphs, or pages

Scriptally Implicit Comprehension: Comprehension requiring considerable use of prior knowledge in combination with information in text

Critical Thinking and Reasoning: Reasoned, reflective thinking that is focused on deciding what to believe or do, drawing inferences or conclusions

Argumentations: Taking a position on an issue and arguing for that position on the basis of evidence

Metacognition: Students' understanding of their own thinking

Source: Murphy et al., 2009.

Next is *philosophy for children*, in which students share reading, listening, or viewing with their teacher and devise their own questions. They choose one question that interests them, and with the teacher's help, discuss it together. The teacher encourages students to welcome the diversity of initial views and then involves them in questioning assumptions, developing opinions with supporting reasons, analyzing significant concepts, and applying good reasoning and judgment.

Third is the *Paideia seminar*. This strategy fosters critical and creative thinking through seminar dialogue, intellectual coaching, and mastery of information. It usually involves three steps: (1) a preseminar content preparation session, (2) a seminar to discuss the ideas, and (3) a postseminar process to assess participation and application of ideas.

Fourth is *questioning the author*, which aims to engage students deeply in the process of deriving meaning from text and in questioning the author's position as an expert. The teacher encourages students to pose queries to the author *while* reading a given text, rather than after reading. The queries may look like "What is the author trying to say?" "Why does the author use the following phrase?" or "Does the author explain this clearly?"

Fifth is *instructional conversation*. This strategy resembles a paradox. It is instructional and aims to promote learning but is also conversational in quality, with natural and spontaneous language interactions free from the didactic language normally used in teaching. In an instructional conversation, the teacher listens carefully, makes guesses about students' intended meanings, and adjusts responses to help students better construct knowledge.

Sixth is *junior great books*. Students work with complex ideas and rigorous texts to develop skills in reading, thinking, and communicating. They use interpretive discussions and construct inferential and thematic meanings from the text.

Seventh is *literature circles*, wherein a group of four students collaborates to select a book to read. The teacher assigns each member one of the four roles: (1) discussion director, (2) literary luminary, (3) vocabulary enricher, and (4) checker. In this way, all students are involved deeply in the process.

Eighth is *grand conversation*, which is a strategy that involves authentic, lively talk about text. The teacher initiates the discussion with a big, overarching question or interpretive prompt. The talk pattern is conversational, and the teacher provides authentic responses to students' statements.

The final strategy is *book club*. In this strategy, students choose what to read and establish their own schedule for reading and discussing books. The key for this strategy is having students read for the sheer joy of it.

One technique Murphy et al. (2009) do not touch on is the Socratic seminar, which can be used for both fiction and nonfiction texts. Within the Socratic seminar, it is important to understand the teacher's role.

- Be the facilitator, not the director.
- Pose well-thought-out, open-ended questions.
- Give no response, positive or negative, to students' discussions.
- Pose questions to move discussion past stalemate positions.

The teacher also needs to explain the guidelines to the students if they are not familiar with a Socratic seminar. The guidelines typically include the following.

- The group sits in a circle, allowing all to make eye contact.
- Students must be prepared!
- Everyone must be respectful of all opinions.
- One student speaks at a time.
- Students should direct comments to classmates (not the teacher).
- Disagreement is fine—as long as it is respectful.
- The speaker should support opinions with textual evidence.
- There is no single right answer.

Lengthy and deep discussions are characterized by complex webs of positions, supportive reasons and evidence, and counterarguments against those reasons and evidence, and the Socratic seminar is one way to prompt such discussion.

Even equipped with these strategies, however, it's helpful to know how to start an engaging conversation with students. Based on the work of Nonye Alozie and Claire Mitchell (2014), William Ewens (1986), and Hale and City (2006), we've put together several easy approaches for beginning a class discussion.

- Start the discussion by posing a broad, open-ended, thematic question that has no obvious right or wrong answer but that genuinely puzzles students and will stimulate thought.

- Begin with a concrete, common experience; a newspaper story; a film; a slide; a demonstration; or a role play.

- Analyze a specific problem. Ask students to identify all possible aspects of the topic or issue under consideration.

- Be benignly disruptive. Start the discussion with a controversy by either causing disagreement among students over an issue or by stating objectively both sides of a controversial topic.

- Help students start to think about what they will learn, and help them access their prior knowledge and understanding of a topic.

- Come to a consensus on the rules for participation, listening, and acceptable ways of interacting. It is important to clarify that students are supposed to address each other with statements and questions rather than directing them to the teacher.

- Establish, or have students brainstorm, accepted criteria for evidence and ways of reasoning. Clarify how the evaluation of the learning and the process will work.

Consider a ninth-grade English teacher's reflection of her lesson using discussion.

> Our discussion lesson on *Romeo and Juliet* had a theme of decisions and consequences. This was the third time this year we had a full discussion lesson. I reviewed a few slides with students at the beginning of the lesson so they remember the rules, and I included the prompts for student discussions on the last slide. I've found that the students enjoy the discussion, though at first it is difficult to get them to speak up. Students using graphic organizers to take notes during their reading (such as the bubble maps on the characters in *Romeo and Juliet*) are more prepared and better able to discuss. Some students have complained that they would rather just talk and not have to cite their evidence in the text, but I have explained to them that this is English class, so citing from the text is the purpose—we're not just here to

discuss philosophy (although that can be part of it). I think this type of discussion is great for students to practice their critical thinking and communication skills.

Compared to one-way lecturing, discussion is an effective way to encourage greater levels of student participation. High-quality discussion also means that students have time to reflect and prepare thought-provoking comments.

Techniques for Improving a Discussion

Once the discussion has started, there are several techniques teachers can use to improve it. Here, we synthesize and present a number of practice tips to help facilitate classroom discussion (Alozie & Mitchell, 2014; Barton, 1995; Henning, McKeny, Foley, & Balong, 2012; van Drie & Dekker, 2013; Worsley, 1975). For instance, when introducing listening strategies to students, the teacher mentally prepares them to listen by encouraging them to consider the context of the upcoming discussion and to establish a purpose or goal for listening. The students stay in communication when another person is talking by actively signaling their listening engagement both nonverbally and verbally.

It's important to note that because students usually need time to think before speaking, the teacher should wait until a student breaks the silence instead of rephrasing or asking a new question. Similarly, aggressive students tend to monopolize discussions, while teachers need to call on shy students. To avoid these scenarios, the teacher can ask an overly talkative student to help by remaining silent. In addition, it is usually easier for shy students to speak in small groups than large ones, and once students have spoken in small-group situations, they will be less reluctant to do so in a larger group. With shy students, teachers can provide cues, give hints, suggest strategies, or draw attention to salient features or particular points of interest to support students as they get into the discussion. Teachers should also assure students that there is no one right answer. Most students are accustomed to discussion situations in which there is a single correct answer or conclusion, and once they realize that there are multiple correct answers, they will be less timid about responding creatively.

Students need to feel that their opinions are valued. If a student makes an astute point that is ignored by the class, the teacher should point it out. Teachers should promote an appreciative atmosphere in the classroom;

everyone—teachers and students alike—should value and really listen to what students say. Along those same lines, the discussions should be relevant to students' lives and concerns. Teachers cannot and need not make everything seem immediately relevant, but whenever possible, they should apply the field of inquiry under discussion to everyday living.

It's important to maintain a collective environment to promote student responsibility and orchestrate turn-based discourse. An effective teacher reformulates questions and interpretations when needed or recaps and elaborates on perspectives to deepen the discussion. One way to keep the ball rolling is to allow breakout sessions in which students in pairs or small groups gather their thoughts about a particular concept or argument.

While the students are in the midst of a discussion, the teacher can move to the back of the room or out of students' line of sight to encourage student-to-student interaction, all while continually monitoring behaviors that may interfere with discussion. For instance, the teacher can keep track of student responses with verbal summaries or use of a public document, such as a chart on the SMART Board, overhead display, or dry-erase board. Or he or she can also use graphic organizers to synthesize student contributions while maintaining instructional focus on a certain new concept. This approach usually encourages both student listening and reflection.

These techniques make classroom discussion effective and more manageable. They allow teachers to establish a learning-centered climate characterized by active engagement, dialogue, and multiway communication. They can also foster extensive collaboration between students and teachers for higher levels of reflective and critical thinking and creative problem solving.

Summary

By verbalizing ideas and opinions during discussion, students not only deepen their understanding of subject content but also learn the important life skill of communication. Through discussion, the talk in classroom is no longer a monologue; students actively learn from each other. In fact, successful discussion prompts students to continuously refine, articulate, and synthesize their knowledge.

To close the chapter, we include several handouts to help teachers effectively integrate discussions into the classroom. In the handout "Types of Student Discussions,"

we look at the nine methods that Murphy et al. (2009) reference. There are many approaches to organizing student discussion around text, and various types of student discussion impact learning outcomes differently (such as text comprehension versus higher-order critical thinking). We recommend that teachers evaluate the students' learning needs and select the method that is best aligned with the learning objectives.

To further the use of a Socratic seminar, we've included a rubric on page 11 that defines levels of performance for students and clearly identifies the skills, knowledge, understanding, and conduct teachers expect students to demonstrate. The rubric may overwhelm students new to Socratic seminars, so more explanation may give students a better understanding of expectations.

Finally, we include the "Student Self-Assessment of Discussion" handout (page 13). Students themselves are critical to the success of student-centered discussions. At the end of the discussion, the teacher can encourage students to reflect on what they've done well and what they can improve. This tool provides a sample format for student self-assessment.

Types of Student Discussions

Strategy	Description	Decision
Critical-analytic		
Collaborative reasoning	In this strategy, "the teacher poses a central question deliberately chosen to evoke varying points of view. Students adopt a position on the issue and generate reasons that support their position. Using the text, as well as personal experiences and background knowledge, students proceed to evaluate reasons, to consider alternative points of view, and to challenge the arguments of others." (Murphy et al., 2009, p. 742)	☐ Appropriate ☐ Not Appropriate
Philosophy for children	Students share reading, listening, or viewing with their teacher and devise their own questions. They choose one question that interests them and, with the teacher's help, discuss it. The teacher encourages students to welcome the diversity of initial views and then involves them in questioning assumptions, developing opinions with supporting reasons, analyzing significant concepts, and applying good reasoning and judgment.	☐ Appropriate ☐ Not Appropriate
Paideia seminar	This strategy fosters critical and creative thinking through seminar dialogue, intellectual coaching, and mastery of information. It usually involves three steps: a preseminar content preparation, a seminar to discuss the ideas, and a postseminar process to assess participation and application of ideas.	☐ Appropriate ☐ Not Appropriate
Efferent		
Questioning the author	This strategy aims to engage students deeply in the process of deriving meaning from text and in questioning the author's position as an expert. The teacher encourages students to pose queries to the author *while* reading a given text rather than after reading. The queries may look like "What is the author trying to say?," "Why does the author use the following phrase?," or "Does the author explain this clearly?"	☐ Appropriate ☐ Not Appropriate
Instructional conversation	This strategy resembles a paradox. It is instructional and aims to promote learning but is also conversational in quality, with natural and spontaneous language interactions free from the didactic characteristic of language normally used for teaching. In the instructional conversation, the teacher listens carefully, makes guesses about students' intended meanings, and adjusts responses to help students better construct knowledge.	☐ Appropriate ☐ Not Appropriate

page 1 of 2

Strategy	Description	Decision
Junior great books	Students work with complex ideas and rigorous texts to develop skills in reading, thinking, and communicating. They use interpretive discussions and construct inferential and thematic meanings from the text.	☐ Appropriate ☐ Not Appropriate
Expressive		
Literature circles	A group of four students selects a book to read. The teacher assigns each member one of the four roles: (1) discussion director, (2) literary luminary, (3) vocabulary enricher, and (4) checker. In this way, all students are involved deeply in the process.	☐ Appropriate ☐ Not Appropriate
Grand conversation	This strategy involves authentic, lively talk about text. The teacher initiates the discussion with a big, overarching question or interpretive prompt. The talk pattern is conversational, and the teacher provides authentic responses to students' statements.	☐ Appropriate ☐ Not Appropriate
Book club	Students choose what to read and establish their own schedule for reading and discussing books. The key for this strategy is having students read for the sheer joy of it.	☐ Appropriate ☐ Not Appropriate

Source: Adapted from Murphy, P. K., Wilkinson, I. A. G., Soter, A. O., Hennessey, M. N., & Alexander, J. F. (2009). Examining the effects of classroom discussion on students' comprehension of text: A meta-analysis. Journal of Educational Psychology, 101*(3), 740–764.*

Instructional Strategies for Effective Teaching © 2016 Solution Tree Press • solution-tree.com
Visit **go.solution-tree.com/instruction** to download this page.

Socratic Seminar Rubric

	Does Not Meet Standard 1	Approaching Standard 2	Meets Standard 3	Exceeds Standard 4
Conduct	• Displays little respect for the learning process; interrupts frequently • Takes advantage of minor distractions • Uses inappropriate discussion skills • Speaks about issues not related to the ideas under discussion; arrives unprepared	• Participates and expresses a belief that his or her ideas are important in understanding the text • May make insightful comments but is either too forceful or too shy and does not contribute to the progress of the conversation • Tends to debate rather than engage in dialogue	• Generally shows composure but may display impatience with contradictory or confusing ideas • Comments, but does not necessarily encourage others to participate • May tend to address only the teacher	• Demonstrates respect for the learning process • Has patience with different opinions and complexity • Shows initiative by asking others for clarification • Brings others into the conversation • Moves the conversation forward • Addresses others in a civil manner, using a collegial and friendly tone
Speaking and Reasoning	• Is extremely reluctant to participate even when called on • Comments in an off-topic or irrelevant way • Mumbles or expresses incomplete ideas • Takes little to no account of previous comments or important ideas in the text	• Responds to questions but may have to be called on • Has read the text but not put much effort into preparing ideas • Comments in a way that takes details into account, but the comments do not flow logically in the conversation	• Responds to questions voluntarily • Comments in a way that shows an appreciation for the text but not an appreciation for the subtler points within it • Writes comments that are logical but not connected to other speakers • Shares ideas interesting enough that others respond to them	• Understands questions before answering • Cites evidence from text • Expresses thoughts in complete sentences • Moves conversation forward • Makes connections among ideas • Resolves apparent contradictory ideas • Considers others' viewpoints • Avoids poor logic

Instructional Strategies for Effective Teaching © 2016 J. H. Stronge • solution-tree.com
Visit **go.solution-tree.com/instruction** to download this page.

	Does Not Meet Standard 1	Approaching Standard 2	Meets Standard 3	Exceeds Standard 4
Listening	• Appears uninvolved in the seminar • Writes comments that display complete or significant misinterpretation of other participants' comments	• Appears to find some ideas unimportant while responding to others • May display confusion due to inattention • Takes few notes during the seminar in response to ideas and comments	• Generally pays attention and responds thoughtfully to ideas and questions of other participants • Absorption in own ideas may distract the participant from ideas of others	• Pays attention to details • Writes notes • Takes responses of all participants into account • Listens to others respectfully by making eye contact with the speaker and waiting her or his turn to speak • Points out faulty logic respectfully
Reading	• Is unprepared for the seminar • Is unfamiliar with important words, phrases, and ideas in the text • Takes no notes or marks no questions in the text • Makes no attempt to get help with difficult material	• Appears to have read or skimmed the text but shows little evidence of serious reflection prior to the seminar • Shows difficulty with vocabulary • Mispronounces important words • Key concepts misunderstood	• Has read the text and comes with good understanding	• Thoroughly familiar with the text • Has written notations • Highlights key words, phrases, and ideas

Instructional Strategies for Effective Teaching © 2016 J. H. Stronge • solution-tree.com

Visit **go.solution-tree.com/instruction** to download this page.

Student Self-Assessment of Discussion

Activity	Poor	Fair	Good
Came to class prepared with notes and sections of the book or reading material bookmarked			
Shared and defended my ideas and opinions			
Asked for clarification when necessary			
Asked higher-level questions of other students			
Spoke to all participants and was heard clearly			
Thought before questioning or answering			
Referred directly to the text and reading material			
Made connections to other speakers' comments; built on ideas and opinions contributed by others			
Did not interrupt and waited patiently for a turn to speak			
Listened actively			

Activity	Poor	Fair	Good
Wrote down thoughts and questions			
Respected others' opinions			
Actively sought to involve others in the discussion			
Developed a deep understanding of the topic discussed			

The goals for this discussion were:

1.

2.

3.

How well did I achieve these goals?

The most rewarding thing about this discussion was:

The most challenging thing about this discussion was:

The next time I am part of a similar discussion, I will make the following changes.

Chapter 2

Concept Attainment

Zero and absolute zero—these are complicated concepts to master for young learners and old learners alike. To help them, effective teachers continually seek ways to make connections among relevant concepts. Grouping, organizing, categorizing, sense making—in essence, developing concepts for understanding the world—are critical aspects of learning for all students, and effective teachers understand the importance of concept building for any subject and in any context.

A concept can be defined as "a set of specific objects, symbols, or events that are grouped together or categorized on the basis of shared characteristics, called attributes" (Holt & Kysilka, 2006, p. 309), so one can think of concepts as the building blocks of education. An effective teacher aims virtually everything he or she does at developing student understanding of a concept and then applying and building on those concepts. In that vein, this chapter explores concept attainment as an instructional method to help students develop skills for inductive and deductive thinking while learning subject matter in a constructive and meaningful way.

What Research Says About Concept Attainment

The research interest on concept attainment started in the 1980s. Robert Tennyson and Martin Cocchiarella (1986) find that concept attainment not only helps students learn subject content but also helps them acquire procedural knowledge and metacognitive skills. Specifically, they summarize the following four methods of research-based teaching concepts.

1. **Definition:** Provide or develop a rule or generality that verbally states the structure of the critical attributes. (Example: Provide the best examples of igneous, sedimentary, and metamorphic rock, and provide direct definitions.)

2. **Expository instances:** Present and explain how to systematically classify examples and non-examples according to variable attributes, thereby making statements to elaborate on the concept. (Example: Explicitly direct students to compare and contrast the examples of igneous, sedimentary, and metamorphic rock.)

3. **Interrogatory instances:** Use questioning to encourage a compare and contrast approach, direct students to identify examples and non-examples, and have them make inferences about the concept by themselves. (Example: Prompt students to categorize the rocks into igneous, sedimentary, or metamorphic groupings based on their knowledge of best examples.)

4. **Attribute elaboration:** Encourage analysis of the critical attributes in expository instances and feedback on the critical attributes in interrogatory instances. (Example: Focus students' attention in a given example, say metamorphic rock, on its specific and unique characteristics, such as texture.)

Similarly, Ok-Choon Park (1984) examines the effectiveness of two concept-teaching strategies.

1. **Classical-attribute-identification strategy:** Facilitate the identification process of critical attributes of a concept. (Example: Use an analytically organized list of critical attributes of igneous, sedimentary, and metamorphic rock.)

2. **Example-comparison strategy:** Facilitate the formation and elaboration process of a prototype concept. (Example: Guide students to compare and contrast examples of igneous, sedimentary, and metamorphic rock.)

Park's (1984) findings indicate that students who use the classical-attribute-identification strategy have more on-task engagement time and better learning performance *during instruction* than those using the example-comparison strategy, but the former students require more time to complete the instructional unit. The findings also show that students using the example-comparison strategy have better learning performance *after instruction* and exhibit better prototype memory formation, which results in a higher degree of retention. Thus, Park (1984) suggests that incorporating both strategies into concept instruction might lead to optimal student learning results. We echo this recommendation.

Studies also find that concept attainment is effective in improving meaningful acquisition of concepts. For instance, a 2013 study by Amit Kumar and Madhu Mathur notes that students instructed with concept attainment outperform those who do not use a formal concept approach (by a mean score of 85.60 versus 65.57) in acquisition of physics concepts. Another study (Fox & Sullivan, 2007) finds that students who practice classification of examples and non-examples are better at identifying new instances of the abstract concepts than students who do not.

There are still other studies that focus on the impact of incorrect examples on student concept learning. For instance, Tim Heemsoth and Aiso Heinze (2014) find that high-achieving sixth-grade students could benefit from incorrect examples when learning the concept of fractions; however, students with low prior achievement learned more from correct examples. In many cases, it is easy to explain why a correct answer is correct, while explaining why an answer is incorrect forces students to confront the inadequacies of the solution. Students of low prior knowledge may find this cognitive process demanding and may demonstrate just as many misconceptions as being exposed to correct examples. However, another study finds that comparing correct and incorrect examples is beneficial for students with low prior learning, even in early stages of the learning process (Durkin & Rittle-Johnson, 2012). After all, it is natural for students to have misconceptions as they learn, and one powerful way to teach them is to find the errors in their thinking and apply meaningful learning strategies to address those errors (Gür & Barak, 2007).

How to Move From Research to Practice

Teachers can use concept attainment to help students inductively develop an abstract, generic idea by using pattern recognition and categorizing skills and then deductively apply the concept in new situations (Pritchard, 1994). More specifically, the strategy, as proposed by Jerome Bruner, aims to build understanding of a concept; it is not only concerned with what a concept is but also the process of how it is acquired (as cited in Boulware & Crow, 2008), and students explore examples as well as non-examples of a concept. By using inductive reasoning, teachers encourage students to apply the attributes to analyze other similar and dissimilar examples before the concept is categorized or named (Boulware & Crow, 2008). Thus, concept attainment is "the search for and testing of attributes that can be used to distinguish exemplars from nonexemplars of various categories" (Joyce, Weil, & Calhoun, 2004, p. 62). Overall, concept attainment is an excellent way to provide opportunities for students to practice inductive reasoning and improve their concept-building strategies.

Preparing to Incorporate Concept Attainment Into the Classroom

The concept attainment approach can nurture awareness of alternative perspectives, sensitivity to logical reasoning in communication, and a tolerance for ambiguity. Peter Martorella (1999) suggests a planning guide for teaching concepts.

> To initiate the process of teaching a concept, you need to ask yourself several basic questions: Do educators and subject matter specialists suggest the concept be taught? Should a student receive systematic instruction in the concept, or is it more appropriately acquired through informal means? Is there a sufficient agreement on the critical attributes . . . to have a basis for designing instructions? Assuming answers are yes to these questions, you are ready to move on to the next phase of instructional planning using the following inventory:

1. What name is commonly applied to the concept? (Example: lake)

2. What is a statement of the concept's rule or definition (the arrangement of its critical attributes)? (Example: body of water surrounded by land on all sides)

3. What are the essential characteristics of critical attributes of the concept based on your readings and reference sources? (Example: land, water, surroundings)

4. What are some noncritical attributes typically associated with the concept? (Example: size, location, depth)

5. What is an example that best or most clearly represents the most typical case of the concept? (Example: aerial photo clearly showing all the features of a lake)

6. What are some other interesting and learner-relevant examples of cases of the concept that you can use in its explanation? (Example: local lakes, mountain lakes, desert lakes)

7. What are some contrasting nonexamples of the concept that will help clarify and illustrate the concept? (Example: ocean, stream)

8. What are some cues, questions, or directions that you can employ to call attention to criteria attributes and noncriterial attributes in the concept examples? (Example: "Look at all the points where the water meets the land.") (as cited in Holt & Kysilka, 2006, p. 311)

Teachers use these steps to facilitate the conceptual types of learning and to adjust how much control they delegate to the students based on what is needed in the learning. For instance, the process can be teacher directed as the teacher explicitly elaborates on the elements of a concept, or it can be student directed by giving students the control to explore and transfer the attainment activity to real-life settings.

Another approach, identified by Bruce Joyce and colleagues (2004), implements concept attainment in a classroom via three linear stages (Joyce et al., 2004). Phase one includes the presentation of data and the identification of the concept. The teacher first presents labeled data to the students—for instance, a set of poems. The teacher labels them *positive* or *exemplars* if they contain characteristics or attributes of the concept being taught or *negative* or *non-exemplars* if they do not contain the attributes of the concept. Students compare the attributes of exemplars and non-exemplars and then develop and test hypotheses about the nature of the category. Through this process, they state the rules or definitions of the concepts according to their essential attributes (their hypotheses are not confirmed at the moment).

Phase two involves testing the attainment of the concept. Students identify additional unlabeled examples as exemplars or non-exemplars. The teacher confirms or disconfirms these hypotheses, names the concept, and restates definitions according to essential attributes. He or she then directs students to generate their own examples.

In the final phase, students describe their thoughts about the learning exercise and discuss the role of hypotheses and attributes. Through discussions, they reflect on their process and analyze the strategies they used to attain the concepts. For teachers, questions that deserve exploration include: What happened when students did not confirm their hypotheses? Did students change strategies?

Assessing Student Learning of Concept Attainment

Formative assessment is integral to concept attainment. Teachers need to practice assessment, especially observational assessment, throughout each phase of a lesson. Concept attainment is quite straightforward, and students progress to the next phase only when they attain the requirements of the prior phase at a satisfactory level. For example, when using the Joyce et al. (2004) approach, teachers ask students to compare and justify the attributes of different examples during the presentation phase. Teachers then determine whether students can identify and articulate the critical attributes. During the testing phase, teachers create opportunities for students to demonstrate their ability to discriminate between exemplars and non-exemplars and generalize the concept to new instances. Teachers also listen as students share their hypotheses, confirm or disconfirm these hypotheses, and reinforce the essential attributes. In the final analysis phase, teachers ascertain students' critical thinking and reasoning abilities by listening to them self-reflect on the learning process (Boulware & Crow, 2008).

After students have completed the three phases, teachers check to see if all students have grasped the concept by instructing them individually or in groups to complete follow-up activities. Examples of activities include (Boulware & Crow, 2008):

- Asking them to explain the concept in their own words
- Generating a list of ideas and thoughts that might include synonyms, examples, or applications of the concept
- Drawing illustrations related to the concept
- Completing graphic organizers to show the relationship of the concept to the examples and non-examples presented
- Making real-world connections

These activities are also particularly useful for assessing student conceptual learning as teachers use the Martorella model (1999). In essence, concept attainment can be a great evaluation tool to determine whether students have mastered important ideas introduced earlier (Joyce et al., 2004). It quickly reveals the depth of students' understanding and reinforces their previous knowledge. In addition, it can open up new conceptual areas by initiating a sequence of individual or group inquiries.

Summary

Learning concepts are an integral part of curriculum. They are crucial not only for acquiring content knowledge but also for developing students' skills to categorize, generalize, and establish the relationship between an abstract idea and referents. Concept attainment is a specific instruction approach for teaching concepts. The core of the concept attainment method is identifying and understanding essential attributes versus nonessential attributes and exemplars versus non-exemplars.

We've designed the handout "Concept Attainment Worksheet" to help students construct a personal understanding of a new concept. The worksheet helps students organize their notes and provides a visual as they learn to distinguish the essential attributes from the nonessential attributes of a concept while they compare exemplars and non-exemplars.

As discussed earlier, teachers need to incorporate checkpoints in each of the phases of learning. We adapted the handout "Concept Attainment Assessment" (page 20) from the work of Beverly Boulware and Mary Lynn Crow (2008). It lays out the criteria to assess the depth of students' conceptual understanding. Students

move to the next phase only once they have attained an acceptable level at the previous phase.

Teacher support and guidance play an important part in the concept attainment process. The teacher not only establishes the exemplars and non-exemplars for students to consider but also provides specific, concrete, and corrective feedback so students develop a conceptual understanding in tandem with accepted understanding. The handout "Concept Attainment Teacher Self-Assessment" (page 21) offers a number of questions to help teachers reflect on the quality of their support while teaching conceptual knowledge.

Concept Attainment Worksheet

Essential attributes:

Non-essential attributes:

Concept:

Exemplars:

Non-exemplars:

Definition given by the teacher:

Definition in my own words:

Concept Attainment Assessment

Phase	Developing	Acceptable	Exemplary
1. Presentation and identification of the concept	• Identifies most essential attributes of the concept	• Identifies the attributes • Provides a definition of the concept	• Identifies the essential and nonessential attributes • Provides a definition of the concept incorporating the essential attributes
2. Testing of the concept	• Identifies additional examples provided by the teachers as yes or no in classification	• Engages in real-world applications involving personal life experiences	• Engages in real-world connections involving personal experiences • Tests and evaluates the hypotheses by applying the new understanding to a novel or extension task
3. Analysis of thinking and reasoning strategies	• Analyzes thinking and reasoning strategies	• Describes his or her thinking • Analyzes correct and incorrect hypotheses	• Engages in analyzing the types of hypotheses shared in the learning experience

Source: Adapted from Boulware, B. J., & Crow, M. L. (2008). Using the concept attainment strategy to enhance reading comprehension. The Reading Teacher, 61*(6), 491–495.*

Instructional Strategies for Effective Teaching © 2016 Solution Tree Press • solution-tree.com

Visit **go.solution-tree.com/instruction** to download this page.

Concept Attainment Teacher Self-Assessment

The following questions help you self-assess your use of concept attainment.

Planning

- Did I pick an important concept in the subject matter to use the concept attainment strategy?
- Did I communicate the learning objectives with clarity at the beginning?
- Have I selected enough exemplars and non-exemplars for students to test their hypotheses with? Were they sequenced in an optimal way?

Implementation

- How did I scaffold students' concept attainment? Did I provide opportunities for student discovery as well as for teacher elaboration and direction?
- How did I address student misconceptions, such as erroneous conceptions, false opinions, or wrong understandings?
- Did I stretch or extend students' conceptual understanding and application?

Assessment

- How well did I assess the depth of student conceptual understanding?
- Did I provide opportunities for students to reflect on their analyzing and reasoning process?
- Did I provide opportunities for students to apply the new concept to novel instances?

Instructional Strategies for Effective Teaching © 2016 J. H. Stronge • solution-tree.com

Visit **go.solution-tree.com/instruction** to download this page.

Chapter 3

Concept Mapping

For both young and old learners, the adage that a picture paints a thousand words holds true. A picture—a graph, chart, map, or other pictorial representation—does more readily convey meaning than words can. As suggested by figure 3.1 (page 24), complex concepts—and connections among concepts—are easier to understand when one can see the ideas and their relationships to one another. While this concept map may not be simple, imagine what it would be like to explain the concepts and connections presented here in words alone. Concept maps simplify complex and nuanced concepts.

According to Hattie (2009),

> Concept mapping involves the development of graphical representations of the conceptual structure of the content to be learnt. . . . Concept mapping can assist in synthesizing and identifying the major ideas, themes, and interrelationships—particularly for the learners who do not have these organizing and synthesizing skills. (p. 168)

Alone or in combination with other instructional tools, concept mapping can serve a variety of useful purposes (Baitz, 2009; Cheema & Mirza, 2013; Plotnick, 1997).

- Communicating complex ideas
- Stimulating creativity and higher-order thinking
- Organizing conceptual knowledge
- Increasing meaningful learning and assessing understanding
- Organizing and planning learning
- Generating ideas (brainstorming)
- Designing complex structures (long texts, hypermedia, large websites)

- Communicating complex ideas
- Aiding learning by explicitly integrating new and old knowledge
- Assessing understanding or diagnosing misunderstandings

A key advantage of concept mapping is that the teacher can readily integrate it into any other instructional delivery approach. In addition, concept mapping is highly adaptable because visual representation has several advantages over text alone. Because students quickly and easily recognize visual symbols, minimum usage of text makes these images easy to scan for a word, phrase, or general idea. Visual representation allows for development of a holistic understanding that words alone cannot convey (Plotnick, 1997), and concept mapping plays an essential role in teaching and learning by helping learners visualize big and small ideas alike.

What Research Says About Concept Mapping

Phillip Horton and colleagues (1993) conducted a meta-analysis of eighteen studies that examined classroom-based use of concept maps. Generally, these studies find that concept mapping has a positive impact on student achievement. Concept mapping by students in groups (with a mean effect size of 0.88 or a gain of about 31 percentile points) and teacher-prepared maps (with a mean effect size of 0.59 or a gain of about 22 percentile points) are two effective strategies to implement concept mapping in classrooms (Horton et al., 1993). This study also indicates that concept mapping affects students' learning attitudes positively. A 2009 synthesis of research by Hattie finds that concept

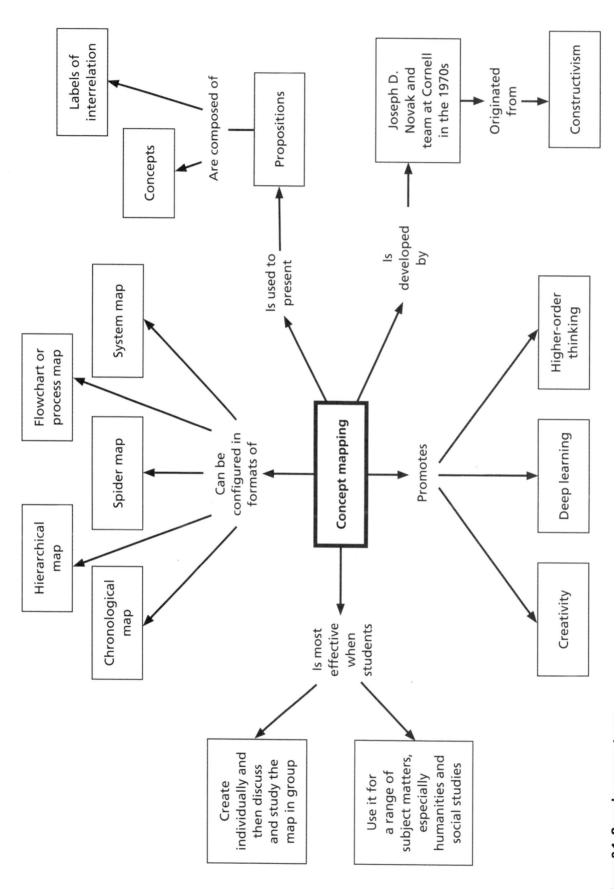

Figure 3.1: Sample concept map.

mapping has an effect size of 0.57 on student achievement. Concept mapping is particularly effective when teachers provide students with the terms for the maps.

The use of concept maps is further bolstered by another meta-analysis of experimental and quasi-experimental studies by John Nesbit and Olusola Adesope (2006), in which an exhaustive search for studies meeting specified design criteria yielded sixty-seven effect sizes from fifty-five studies involving 5,818 participants. The use of concept maps benefits learners across a broad range of educational levels (from K–12 to the postsecondary level), subject areas (from sciences to humanities), and settings (from classroom to laboratory) (Nesbit & Adesope, 2006). The authors find that concept mapping offers greater benefits in subject areas that emphasize verbal knowledge, such as humanities, law, and social studies (with an effect size of 1.265, or a gain of 40 percentile points), than in science, biology, and statistics (with an effect size of 0.522, or a gain of 20 percentile points). They also find that concept mapping is more effective when students individually construct maps and then discuss them in a whole-class activity (with an effect size of 0.955, or a gain of 33 percentile points), rather than just create the maps individually without discussion (with an effect size of 0.119, or a gain of 4 percentile points). Recall that we elaborated on classroom discussion in chapter 1 (page 3). It is worth noting that no instructional strategy is a silver bullet or purported to be a stand-alone. Given the dynamics and specific needs in the classroom, it is not surprising to see that integrating two strategies is more effective than relying on just one.

The 2013 study by Ahmad Cheema and Munawar Mirza analyzes the effect of concept mapping on academic performance of seventh-grade students in science. In this quasi-experimental research, the experimental group was trained to develop concept maps for three weeks. The results show that students taught through concept mapping perform better than students taught through traditional methods. Still more studies find that concept mapping can improve students' reading comprehension in expository science texts (Oliver, 2009) and skills in retrieving and reconstructing knowledge in science (Karpicke & Blunt, 2011). In fact, Kevin Oliver's (2009) study shows that students prefer to read and map rather than read without mapping. The study also finds that students prefer to map in pairs or small groups as compared with mapping alone.

In addition, students experience better learning outcomes when they fill in partially completed teacher-constructed concept maps than when they self-construct maps from scratch (Chang, Sung, & Chen, 2001) or study complete maps constructed by the teachers (Tan, 2000). Kuo-En Chang and colleagues (2001) find that when students engage in scaffolded concept mapping (in which they receive an incomplete framework of an expert concept map as a scaffold with some blank nodes and links), they outperform students who work at self-constructed concept mapping (in which they construct maps freely from scratch with no scaffolding aid, relying merely on a list of concepts and relationships). In a later study, Chang et al. (2002) discovered that if students detect and correct the partially incorrect nodes and links in the expert map (with 40 percent inaccuracy), they demonstrate more improvement in text comprehension and summarization than those who use the scaffolded concept mapping or self-constructed concept mapping.

Another study finds that when cooperative learning incorporates concept mapping, students discuss concepts being taught, collaboratively elaborate on conflicts and reasoning, and experience better individual learning outcomes, particularly when they prepare individually prior to group collaboration (van Boxtel, van der Linden, & Kanselaar, 2000). A 2002 study by Carla van Boxtel, Jos van der Linden, Erik Roelofs, and Gijsbert Erkens also notes that collaborative concept mapping helps students observe the relationships among concepts, reflect on their (mis)understandings, form high-quality explanations of conceptual knowledge, and conduct richer interactive discourse to co-construct the meanings and relationships of the concepts.

How to Move From Research to Practice

We have adapted Joseph Novak and Alberto Cañas's (2008) excellent set of guidelines to help apply concept mapping in the classroom. The following six steps sequentially detail their approach and offer practical, user-friendly advice on how to build, embellish, critique, and refine concept maps.

1. **Begin with a familiar domain of knowledge:** It is important to embed the concept map in a familiar context (such as a segment of a text or a field activity), one narrow and informative enough for learners to identify its hierarchical structure.

2. **Use a focus question to define the issue being mapped:** It is a good idea to construct a focus question to clarify the particular problem or issue the concept map attempts to address. Novice learners of concept maps tend to digress from the focus question to build a concept map that is overly inclusive of loosely integrated components. A well-framed question leads learners to structure their knowledge in a synergic manner and, thus, develop a richer concept map. Using a clear focus question capitalizes on a well-accepted axiom—the first step to learning about something is to ask the right questions.

3. **Identify the key concepts that apply to the knowledge domain:** Given a selected domain and a defined problem, the next step is to identify between fifteen and twenty-five key concepts that apply to the domain. These concepts could be ranked in a column, with the most inclusive concept placed at the top of the list and the most specific one placed at the bottom. Teachers then encourage students to perceive this list as a parking lot; the items on the list will be moved into the concept map, but some may also remain in the parking lot if the students do not see a good connection with other concepts on the map.

4. **Construct a preliminary concept map:** Students can create a preliminary concept map with various techniques. They can write all of the concepts on sticky notes, allowing them to move concepts around easily on a whiteboard or large sheet of paper. Another good option is electronic software developed specifically for concept mapping, which enables mapmakers to easily arrange and conceptualize connections among concepts.

5. **Develop cross-links to connect concepts across subdomains:** Developing cross-links among concepts in different subdomains of knowledge can help students appreciate the interrelationships among areas of the map. Since all concepts can relate to one another in certain ways, it is important for students to recognize the need to be selective when identifying interconnections.

6. **Recognize that a concept map is never finished:** A preliminary concept map usually requires modifications and revisions as students' understanding about the concept deepens. They may need to add new concepts and connections or take out existing ones. A sound concept map usually undergoes a minimum of three revisions. Notepads and computer-based concept mapping software are helpful for multiple revisions.

Amy Benjamin (2003) provides additional advice on how to put concept mapping into practice. She notes that students should draw concept maps quickly—the less self-editing, the better. To encourage students' non-linear thinking, teachers should provide plenty of space and freedom on the page; unlined paper is optimal, as lined paper inhibits nonlinear thinking. Leaving white space allows for ideas to develop later. When creating the scaffolding, the teacher should position the paper horizontally and place the main idea, topic, or issue in the center. It's important to keep the map brief and readable.

To indicate relationships among key concepts, students can use colors, clusters, arrows, shading, and branches. Think in terms of different configurations, such as cloud diagrams (clusters of overlapping circles), tree diagrams, constellations (star patterns), and flowcharts. Students may find some configurations more helpful than others, and providing the choice allows them to take ownership of their understanding. Teachers can also differentiate the process by providing different levels of scaffold for students based on their learning ability or by having students identify designs that are meaningful to them.

One technique is to circle nouns and connect verbs with lines (as illustrated in figure 3.1, page 24). Students can also use different colors and shapes for nodes and links to identify the various types of information and to integrate new concepts with older concepts. In addition, students should think in terms of *who, what, when, where,* and *why* when brainstorming and generating ideas. Think of the concept map as an emergent model—a work in progress. The class should revisit it often to add ideas, make new spin-off maps out of secondary ideas, and discuss any misconceptions that students may have.

Benjamin (2003) also recommends a series of useful criteria for evaluating student concept maps. These four criteria are listed in table 3.1 along with descriptions of how to apply the criteria.

Table 3.1: Criteria and Accompanying Considerations for Evaluating Concept Mapping

Criteria for Evaluating Concept Mapping	Considerations for Applying Criteria
Accuracy of relationships	• Are the relationships accurately named? • Does the space interval between items accurately represent the relationship?
Correct use of terminology	• Did advanced students compose their own terminology list? • Can emergent learners complete a list that has been initiated by the teacher? • Can beginning learners use a list that has been provided for them?
Detail and specificity	• What is the degree of sophistication of the concept map? This should be contingent on the complexity of expected student learning.
Overall organization plan	• Is the concept map systematic, easy to follow, and simple in design?

Source: Adapted from Benjamin, 2003, pp. 85–86.

Concept maps are a great way for students to visualize thinking and make strong connections. In addition, they help teachers ensure that students understand the concept thoroughly and without misunderstandings.

Summary

Students tend to learn better when the new learning is related to and anchored in prior knowledge. Concept mapping prompts learners to reorganize and expand their internal representation of the world, and the nodes and relationships of a concept map make the knowledge explicit and concrete. Learning is about making connections, and concept mapping helps students understand that knowledge is like furniture—it can be arranged and integrated in different ways.

As described earlier, there are many purposes that concept mapping can fulfill and many ways that a teacher can scaffold and structure the task. The handout "Decisions Checklist for Teaching With Concept Maps" (page 28) helps teachers think through their decision making to find the optimal format of concept mapping and align the maps with student learning ability and content objectives.

Concept mapping is considered a type of graphic organizer. The logical structure of the abstract concept determines its configuration. Types of configurations include chronological, hierarchical, flowchart, process, spider, and systems maps. Each has advantages and disadvantages. For instance, flowchart, process, and spider configurations are easy to maneuver, but they do not facilitate higher-order thinking as well as other designs. Chronological and hierarchical maps serve specific structures well but may limit depicting more complicated relationships among concepts. Systems concept maps can facilitate deeper thinking, but students may find them challenging to configure. The handout "Configurations of Concept Maps" (page 29) lays out the major configurations for teachers to choose from.

As noted, teachers can use concept mapping as an assessment tool to monitor students' understanding and skills in organizing and representing knowledge. Thus, we adapted the final handout (page 34) from Benjamin (2003) to serve as a rubric to evaluate student concept mapping when it is used as an assessment.

Decisions Checklist for Teaching With Concept Maps

I am going to use concept maps:

- ☐ To organize and plan learning
- ☐ To generate ideas (brainstorming)
- ☐ To design complex structures (long texts, product of a project)
- ☐ To communicate complex ideas
- ☐ To assist students' writing as a prewriting strategy
- ☐ To facilitate memorization
- ☐ To aid learning by explicitly integrating new and old knowledge
- ☐ To assess students' understanding or diagnose misunderstandings
- ☐ For other reasons: _____

I am going to make concept maps:

- ☐ Open-ended; therefore, I will not provide any preselected concepts
- ☐ More structured; I will give students a concept map template with the following superordinate terms and preselected concepts—

- ☐ Differentiated; I will provide open-ended templates for some students and structured templates for others

I am going to have the students work on concept maps:

- ☐ Individually
- ☐ In pairs
- ☐ In small groups
- ☐ As a whole class

The learning objective of the concept map is to:

Configurations of Concept Maps

Following are five types of concept maps.

Flowchart or Process Map

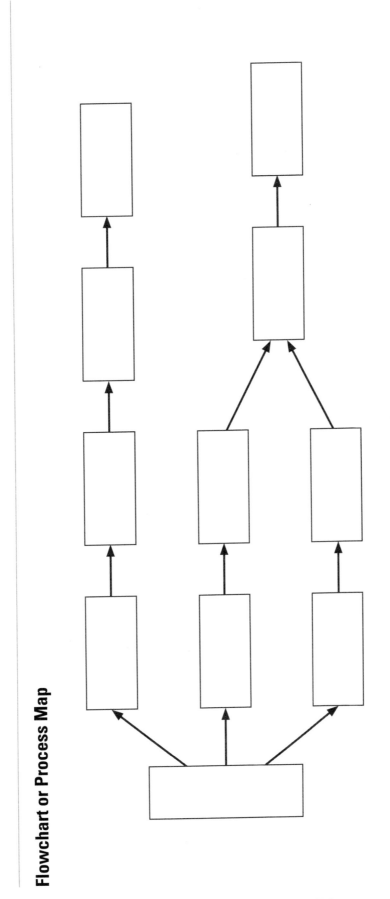

Instructional Strategies for Effective Teaching © 2016 J. H. Stronge • solution-tree.com

Visit **go.solution-tree.com/instruction** to download this page.

Hierarchical Concept Map

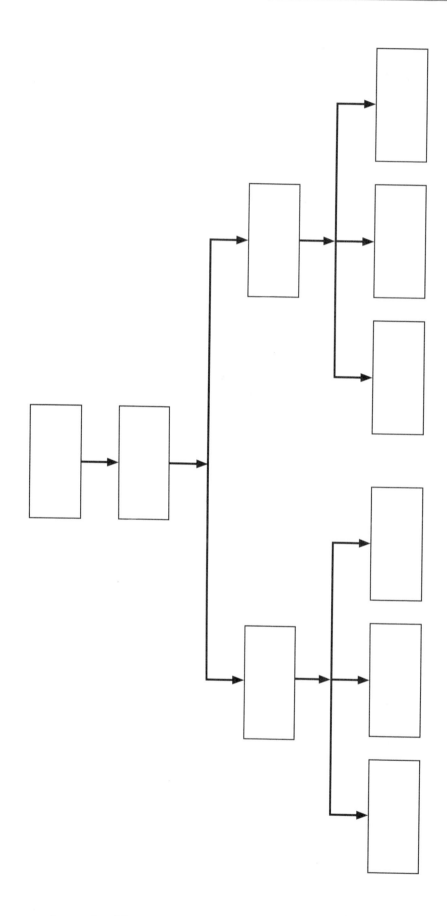

Instructional Strategies for Effective Teaching © 2016 J. H. Stronge • solution-tree.com

Visit **go.solution-tree.com/instruction** to download this page.

Chronological Map

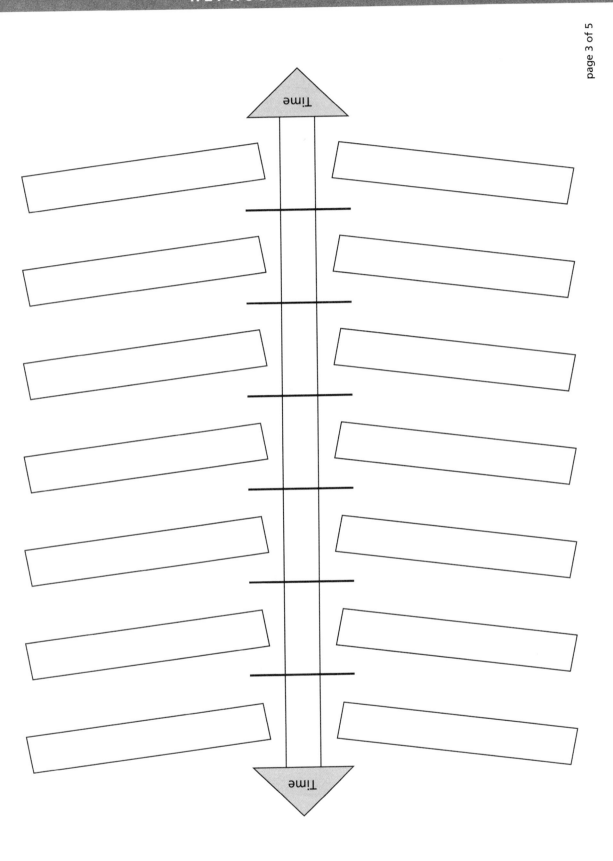

Spider Map

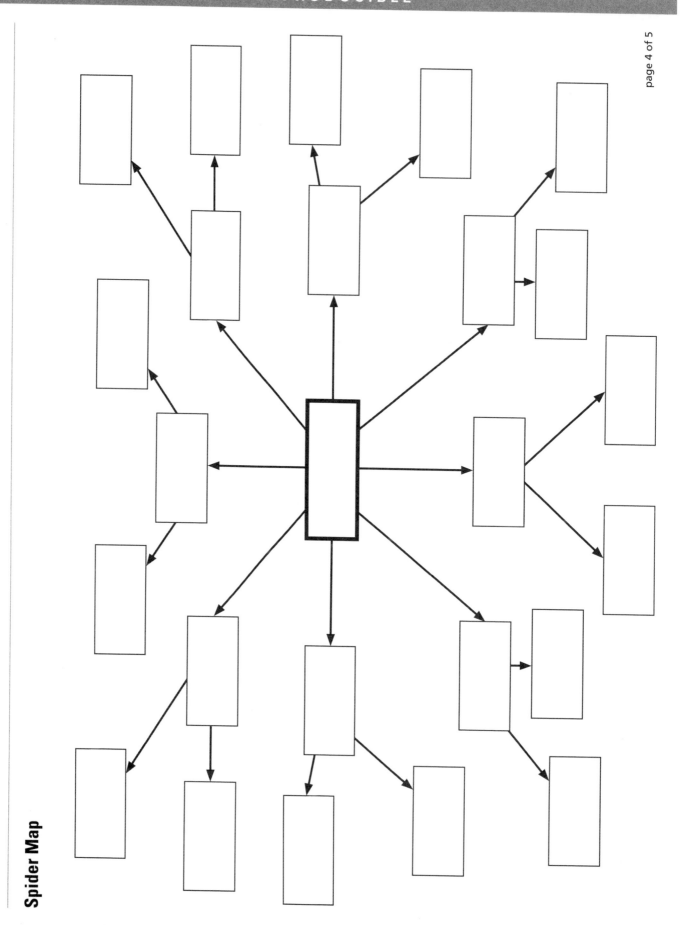

System Map

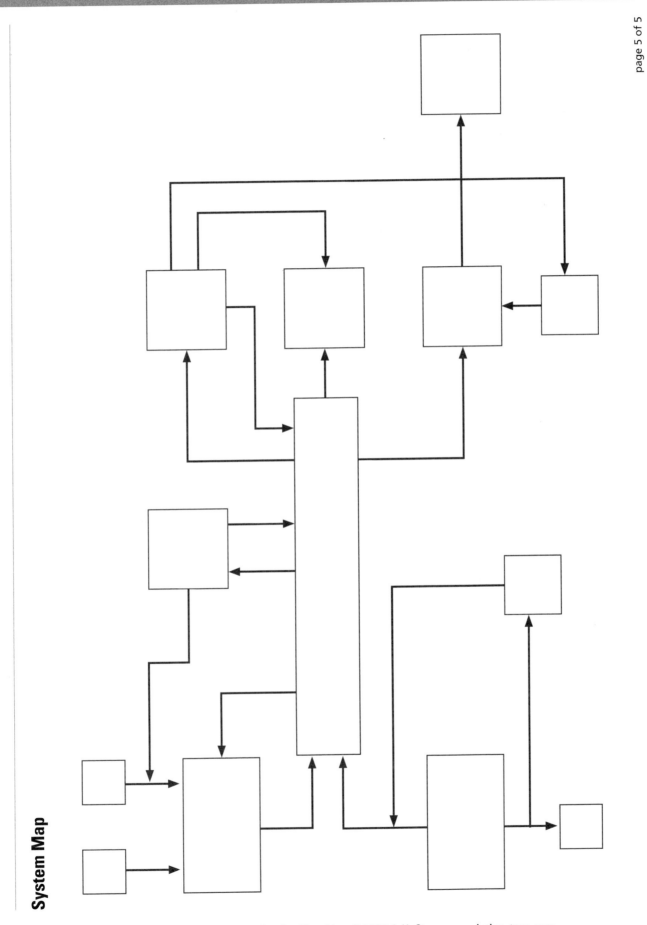

Rubric to Evaluate Student Concept Mapping

Criteria	Guiding Questions	Emerging	Developing	Acquired	Accomplished
Accuracy of relationships	• Are the relationships accurately interlinked? • Do the linking lines and descriptive words between items accurately represent the relationship?				
Correct use of terminology	• Did students include all important terminologies? • Did advanced students compose their own terminology lists? • Can emergent learners complete lists that I initiated? • Can beginning learners use lists that I provided for them?				

Criteria	Guiding Questions	Emerging	Developing	Acquired	Accomplished
Detail and specificity	• What is the degree of sophistication of the concept map? This should be contingent upon the complexity of expected student learning. • Does the map contain relevant hierarchies (visual and conceptual)?				
Overall organization plan	• Is the concept map systematic, easy to follow, and simple in design? • Does the concept map have a clean and appealing design that aids comprehension?				

Additional Comments:

Source: Adapted from Benjamin, A. (2003). Differentiated instruction: A guide for elementary school teachers. Larchmont, NY: Eye on Education.

Chapter 4
Cooperative Learning

According to prominent researchers David Johnson and Roger Johnson (1999a), "cooperative learning is the instructional use of small groups so that students work together to maximize their own and each other's learning. It may be contrasted with competitive and individualistic learning" (p. 5). At its core, cooperative learning encourages students to help each other succeed in shared learning experiences. The synergy students generate in cooperative settings tends to motivate them more than the atmosphere of individualistic, competitive environments. In addition, interaction with fellow students can produce cognitive as well as social complexity, creating mental activity that increases learning more than solitary study (Joyce et al., 2004).

For some people, cooperative learning may simply mean having students work together in small groups. However, when teachers don't appropriately implement and monitor the groups, quality student learning doesn't occur; simply calling any group work cooperative learning is an injustice. For students to realize the potential benefits of cooperative learning, its purpose in the classroom must relate to desired student outcomes, and teachers should implement it using proven models. Thus, this instructional method provides a practical resource to help teachers bring major elements of cooperative learning to life in classrooms.

What Research Says About Cooperative Learning

Johnson and Johnson (1989) conducted a comprehensive review of research related to cooperative learning in which they synthesize the findings from 754 studies. Specifically, they examine the impact of three modes of learning—(1) cooperative, (2) competitive, and (3) individualistic. They find that cooperative learning strategies consistently have larger effects on achievement and productivity. Overall, cooperative learning has an effect size of 0.67 (25 percentile points) compared with competitive learning and an effect size of 0.64 (24 percentile points) compared with individualistic learning. Also, cooperative learning has an effect size of 0.76 (28 percentile points) on student on-task behavior in comparison with competitive learning and an effect size of 1.17 (38 percentile points) when compared with individualistic learning. This study finds in addition that cooperative experiences promote positive attitudes toward learning, with an effect size of 0.57 (22 percentile points) over competitive learning and 0.42 (16 percentile points) over individualistic learning. Furthermore, cooperative learning is positively associated with the following (Johnson & Johnson, 1989).

- Long-term retention of learning
- Enhanced cognitive processing (for example, more higher-level reasoning strategies, more frequent generation of new ideas and solutions)
- Greater transfer of learning to new situations
- Intrinsic motivation and continued motivation to learn
- Development of positive interpersonal relationships (for example, developing caring and committed relationships; establishing and maintaining friendships; and improving productivity, morale, sense of responsibility, and sense of belonging)
- Improved psychological health (for example, higher self-esteem, resiliency, and perseverance)

A number of studies corroborate these research findings. For instance, William Lan and Judi Repman (1995) find that cooperative learning enhances students' enthusiasm for learning and their determination to achieve academic success. Robert Stevens and Robert Slavin (1995a, 1995b) note that it increases the academic achievement of students of all ability levels, and Catherine Mulryan (1995) asserts that it promotes more student time on task and engagement.

Edmund Emmer and Mary Claire Gerwels (2002) conducted interviews and observations of eighteen elementary teachers that reveal "there was considerable variation in the extent to which lessons incorporate major features of [cooperative learning]" (p. 75). According to them, lesson success (as measured by student performance and progress on the lesson's academic task, cooperation within groups, and student engagement) is associated with the greater presence of features like individual or group accountability, teacher monitoring, feedback, and the use of manipulative materials in group work (Emmer & Gerwels, 2002).

Some experimental studies find that cooperative learning positively impacts students' reading comprehension (Khan & Ahmad, 2014) and mathematics achievement (Zakaria, Chin, & Daud, 2010). A study by David Johnson, Roger Johnson, and Cary Roseth (2010) examining cooperative learning in middle schools confirms that cooperation promotes academic achievement (a 0.46 standard deviation increase over competitive learning and a 0.55 standard deviation increase over individualistic learning) and more positive relationships (0.48 and 0.42 standard deviation increases, respectively). However, these positive outcomes occur when teachers carefully structure cooperative learning experiences to include five essential elements: (1) positive interdependence; (2) individual accountability; (3) interactions that give students opportunities to help each other, share resources, and solve problems collaboratively; (4) appropriate use of social skills; and (5) group processing.

In middle schools, the quality of peer relationships accounts for 33 to 44 percent of the variance in student achievement, which makes cooperative learning particularly appealing (Johnson et al., 2010). Hattie's (2009) meta-analysis reveals that cooperative learning has an effect size of 0.54 over competitive learning and 0.59 over individualistic learning. A 2013 meta-analysis by Eva Kyndt et al. finds that cooperative learning has an average effect size of 0.54 on academic achievement,

0.15 on attitudes of learning, and 0.18 on perceptions of the subject. It also finds that effect sizes of studies in cooperative learning are larger in nonlinguistic courses like mathematics and sciences than in social sciences and languages. Interestingly, there is no significant difference between an individual reward method (such as rewarding each group member based on his or her performance of a unique task) and a group reward method (such as rewarding the whole group based on the average of their individual learning performances) in cooperative learning. However, both individual accountability and group goals are essential components of cooperative learning (Kyndt et al., 2013).

Robert Slavin (1995) reviews the research on practical implications of cooperative learning methods in actual classroom use to determine its impact on measures of student achievement. Table 4.1 offers an overview of six of these well-researched and practical cooperative learning methods useful for both elementary and secondary students. It's important to remember that experts consider effect sizes at or above 0.25 educationally significant. The handouts that close this chapter describe in detail each of these cooperative methods.

Teachers play an important role in determining how effective cooperative learning will be. For instance, John Ross (1995) finds that teacher feedback and monitoring are essential to the effectiveness of cooperative learning. When teachers give assessment and feedback to students' performance, students increase the frequency and quality of help seeking and help giving during cooperative learning (Ross, 1995). Robyn Gillies and Michael Boyle (2010) assert that although cooperative learning is known "to be a pedagogical practice that promotes academic achievement and socialization" (p. 933), research has also found the use of cooperative learning has declined and few teachers use recognized forms of cooperation in classrooms. Their research uncovers many difficulties with implementing cooperative learning, such as students socializing during group activities rather than working, teachers failing to manage time effectively, and teachers underestimating the preparation required. Other challenges include deciding on the composition of groups, the types of learning tasks to undertake, the social skills training needed, and the assessment of student work in groups (Gillies & Boyle, 2010). To avoid this decline and to increase student performance, teachers must learn the best ways to incorporate this important instructional method into daily classroom life.

Table 4.1: Cooperative Methods and Mean Effect Sizes

Cooperative Methods	Mean Effect Sizes (on all tests measuring thinking skills, self-esteem, and attitudes toward learning)
Student team achievement divisions	0.32
Teams-games-tournaments	0.38
Jigsaw	0.12
Group investigation	0.06
Structured dyadic methods	0.86

Source: Slavin, 1995.

How to Move From Research to Practice

There are various methods or models to implement cooperative learning in classrooms. Despite shared assumptions and a common framework, they demonstrate different features (such as the degree of structure or teacher control) and processes, and they best serve different learning purposes. For instance, teachers could use the various methods listed in table 4.1: group investigation, student team achievement divisions, the teams-games-tournaments method, the jigsaw method, or structured dyadic methods. Depending on the context, cooperative learning can be relatively informal, as in a jigsaw method in which social dynamics and discussion are more emphasized than well-specified content. The varying details in terms of grouping, group members' roles, the teacher's role, and assessment of student performance among these five models are explained in the handout of "Cooperative Learning Models" (page 43).

No matter what form cooperative learning takes in a classroom, it should have the basic elements listed in table 4.2 (page 40) to be effective.

While student learning goals can be structured to promote cooperative, individualistic, or competitive efforts (Johnson & Johnson, 1999b)—and each goal structure has its place—in cooperative learning, students work together to accomplish shared goals. Although the core of cooperative learning is for students to learn from their peers, the teacher plays a role in establishing a positive interdependent environment, assigning roles, teaching social skills, assessing, and rewarding.

At a minimum, developing a framework for applying cooperative learning in classroom settings requires teachers to:

- Create truly interdependent tasks
- Establish clear goals for group work
- Organize discussions
- Monitor activities to reinforce how students can help one another
- Facilitate frequent evaluations of how work progresses

Additionally, teachers can informally recognize a particular student's strength or ability so that other students may rely on that student for assistance (LePage, Darling-Hammond, & Akar, 2005).

Expanding on the work of Donald Orlich, Robert Harder, Richard Callahan, and Harry Gibson (2001), there are four practical steps to consider when designing and implementing a cooperative learning framework in the classroom. Step 1 is to decide if cooperative learning is the best approach. Make sure that cooperative learning is the right strategy to serve the instructional objectives as well as the needs of individual students. It is important to consider the mix of student abilities in the classroom, especially since students may marginalize their peers with weak task-relevant skills in a group activity. Mulryan (1992) finds that high achievers engage in significantly higher-level attending behavior than do low achievers in cooperative learning situations. Thus, teachers using cooperative instruction must note individual patterns of participation among their students in small groups and take steps to promote active involvement by all students, especially low achievers.

Table 4.2: Elements of Cooperative Learning in Relation to Behaviors

Basic Elements of Cooperative Learning	Student Behaviors	Teacher Behaviors
Positive interdependence	Students work together as a team and have a commitment to others' success as well as their own.	The teacher establishes mutual goals, joint rewards, shared resources, and assigned roles.
Individual and group accountability	The group is accountable for achieving its goals, and each student is accountable for his or her academic progress and task completion.	The teacher assesses the quality and quantity of each group member's contributions and gives the results to the group and the individual.
Promotive interaction	Students work directly with one another, assist one another, share opinions and ideas, and come to a common understanding.	The teacher organizes the seats so that members sit knee to knee and talk through each aspect of the tasks they are working to complete.
Interpersonal and small-group skills	Students develop an array of social skills, including communicating, appreciating different perspectives, decision making, problem solving, and functionally resolving conflicts.	The teacher emphasizes and models social skills (such as building trust or conflict management) purposefully and explicitly in daily work.
Group processing	Groups of students evaluate and discuss how well the group has attained its goals, what did and did not work during the process of group work, and continuous improvement.	The teacher assigns such tasks as listing one action that could be added to make the group work more effective or writing reflective journals about the occurrences during the group collaboration.

Source: Adapted from Johnson & Johnson, 1999a, 1999b.

Step 2 is to plan cooperative learning activities carefully. Successful cooperative learning doesn't occur by happenstance. Rather, the effective use of cooperative learning as a systematic instructional practice requires teachers to plan carefully, including setting academic and social goals.

Step 3 involves selecting and organizing student work groups. Teachers can base cooperative work groups on students' academic skill level, interests, personality characteristics, social skills, or a combination of these factors. When needed, teachers can assign specific roles to each group member, including the following.

- **Group leader:** Facilitates group discussion and makes sure the group sets goals and works to meet them

- **Monitor:** Monitors time on task and ensures that everyone gets equal opportunity to participate

- **Resource manager:** Gathers and organizes materials

- **Recorder:** Keeps a written or taped record of group activities

- **Reporter:** Shares group findings and plans during whole-class discussions

Finally, in step 4, the teacher monitors success. He or she must implement cooperative learning plans with fidelity. The teacher needs to monitor and evaluate progress of both individual students and working groups as a whole.

Johnson and Johnson (1999b) suggest that the steps teachers employ in cooperative learning depend on the key elements that each cooperative learning model reflects. The typologies they offer include those discussed in table 4.3. In *informal work groups*, students work together in temporary, ad hoc groups that last from a few minutes to one class period to achieve joint learning goals. In *formal work groups*, students work together for one or several class sessions to achieve shared learning goals and complete specific tasks and assignments. Finally, in *cooperative groups*, students work together in long-term, heterogeneous cooperative learning groups with stable membership.

Again, table 4.3 shows the versatility of cooperative learning. It can range in length from a few minutes to one class period, or from several weeks to a whole school year. It can be organized on the fly or be stable and routinized. It can result in a graded project or be ungraded. Also, these three types of cooperative learning can be used together. For instance, a teacher can start a lesson

Table 4.3: Types of Cooperative Learning

Types of Cooperative Learning	Steps
Informal work groups	• Plan one or two questions to help students organize, in advance, what they know about the material to be presented. • Create expectations and a mood conducive to learning. • Assign students to pairs or triads, ask them to turn to each other and work collaboratively in answering a question, and ensure each student is cognitively processing the material being taught. • Require students to provide closure to a discussion.
Formal work groups	• Make preinstructional decisions, including formulating objectives, deciding on the size of groups, choosing a method for assigning students to groups, deciding which roles to assign group members, arranging the room, and organizing the materials students need to complete the assignment. • Set the task and the cooperative structure in class, including explaining the academic assignment and criteria for success to students, structuring positive interdependence, discussing individual accountability, and describing expected behaviors during the lesson. • Monitor the groups while they work, and intervene when needed to improve teamwork. • Evaluate student learning and process group functioning, including assessing and evaluating the quality and quantity of student achievement, ensuring that students carefully self-evaluate the effectiveness of their learning groups, having students make a plan for improvement, and encouraging students to celebrate the hard work of group members.
Cooperative groups	• Structure the opening of class meetings to complete routine tasks, such as checking attendance and homework, ensuring members understand previously learned material, and preparing members for the day. • Structure the ending of a class meeting to ensure all members understand the newly learned material, know what homework to do, and are making progress on long-term assignments. • Guide members to help each other learn between classes. • Guide groups to conduct semester- or year-long academic or service projects in the class or the whole school.

with informal work groups, follow up with formal work groups, and end with cooperative groups.

Summary

Learning cooperatively is an important mode of learning, and cooperative learning can take a variety of forms. Fortunately, an extensive research base exists for this instructional strategy. Teachers who wish to use cooperative learning effectively and genuinely should base classroom practices on the ideas validated by research. Cooperative learning is more than having students sit together, and having students who finish their work first help others is not cooperative learning either. A true cooperative learning experience requires division of labor, meaningful interactions, collaborative processing of a task, a sense of interdependence, and individual and group accountability.

There are numerous methods and models for effectively implementing cooperative learning in the classroom, and it would be presumptuous of us to think we have included all of the viable options. However, we designed the handout "Cooperative Learning Models" (page 43) to offer guidance for five solidly researched and field-tested cooperative learning models to employ in classrooms.

In order to make sure students are working toward the same standard, it is helpful to provide a rubric for student self-assessment. Through self-assessment, students can better understand their learning process and actively reflect on their performance. The handout "Cooperative Learning Student Self-Assessment Rubric" (page 46) provides a sample rubric. The first section targets group accountability and the second section targets individual accountability, as Johnson and Johnson (1999a, 1999b) identify. The teacher can adapt the tool as needed to meet specific needs.

Finally, the handout "Cooperative Learning Teacher Reflection" (page 47) provides reflective questions so teachers can assess cooperative learning against the five components proposed by Johnson and Johnson (1999a, 1999b).

Cooperative Learning Models

Following are five different methods to incorporate cooperative learning into the classroom.

Group Investigation

The instructional procedure for implementing the group investigation method involves three processes: (1) investigation, (2) interaction, and (3) interpretation (Sharan & Sharan, 1992). Major features of this approach include the growth of students' initiatives in asking questions to direct research, cooperatively planning the group's research process, and participating in the group's preparation of a final product. These features unfold over a period of time, during which the class (organized into small groups) pursues the investigation of the topic under study, and implementation follows these general guidelines (Sharan & Sharan, 1992).

1. The teacher presents a broad topic for study, and the class determines subtopics and organizes into small research groups.

2. Groups plan their investigation and the roles of each group member.

3. Groups carry out their investigation, during which students acquire, analyze, and evaluate information. Groups assemble, share knowledge, and plan how to prepare their final product.

4. Groups develop a final report and plan to present their findings to the class.

5. Groups make their presentations.

6. Student committees and the teacher evaluate the presentations collaboratively.

For our purposes, group investigation is a(n):

_____ Optimal match

_____ Acceptable match

_____ Poor match or not a match

Student Team Achievement Divisions

In student team achievement divisions (STAD), students are assigned to four-member learning teams that are mixed in performance level, gender, and ethnicity. The teacher presents a lesson, and students study together within their teams to make sure all team members have mastered the lesson. Then, all students take individual quizzes on the material independently without assistance from one another. Students' quiz scores are compared to their own past averages, and individual improving scores are awarded based on the degree to which each student can meet or exceed his or her own earlier performance. The teacher combines the individual points to form team scores and uses certificates or other rewards to recognize teams that meet certain criteria. The whole cycle of activities, from teacher presentation to team study to quiz, usually takes three to five class periods. A regular cycle of STAD instructional activities can be summarized as follows (Slavin, 1991, 1995).

1. **Teach:** Present the lesson.

2. **Team study:** Students work on worksheets in their teams to master the material.

3. **Test:** Students take individual quizzes.

4. **Individual improvement scores:** Calculate students' improvement points based on how much their quiz scores exceed their baseline scores.

5. **Team recognition:** Compute team scores based on team members' improvement scores, and give certificates or other recognition to high-scoring teams.

For our purposes, student team achievement divisions are a(n):

_____ Optimal match

_____ Acceptable match

_____ Poor match or not a match

Teams-Games-Tournaments

The teams-games-tournaments (TGT) method relies on the same teacher presentation and teamwork as in STAD, but "replaces the individual student quizzes with weekly or after-unit tournaments in which students play academic games with members of the other teams to contribute points to their team scores" (Slavin, 1996, p. 22). Students then play the games at three-person tournament tables with others of similar performance levels. After the first tournament, students switch tables depending on their performance in the previous tournament. The winner at each table advances to the next highest table, the second scorer stays at the same table, and the third scorer moves to the next lowest table. The winner of each tournament table brings the same number of points to his or her team. At the end of the entire tournament, the teacher compiles team scores. Teammates assist each other in preparing for the tournament by studying worksheets and explaining problems to each other. As in STAD, high-performing teams earn certificates or other kinds of team rewards (Slavin, 1991, 1995).

For our purposes, teams-games-tournaments are a(n):

_____ Optimal match

_____ Acceptable match

_____ Poor match or not a match

Jigsaw

In the jigsaw method, the teacher assigns students to three-to-six-member home teams to work on sectioned academic materials or assignments. Each member of the group is assigned a section to study; he or she becomes an expert. Experts then convene and form expert groups in which they discuss the information and decide on the best way to present the material to members of their home teams. Then, the home teams reconvene and each member teaches the others about his or her specific section. The teacher administers quizzes and gives teams recognition and rewards in the same fashion as STAD (Slavin, 1991).

For our purposes, jigsaw is a(n):

_____ Optimal match

_____ Acceptable match

_____ Poor match or not a match

Structured Dyadic Methods

Structured dyadic methods involve pairs of students teaching each other. One of the most widely used methods is classwide peer tutoring, in which the teacher pairs students to tutor one another using a simple study procedure. For instance, tutors present problems to their tutees. If the tutees answer correctly, they earn points. If otherwise, the tutor provides the correct answer, and the tutee writes the answer three times, rereads a sentence correctly, or corrects his or her errors. The tutors and tutees alternate roles every few minutes. As a result, the teacher awards students points for systematically implementing good tutoring behaviors (Slavin, 1995).

For our purposes, structured dyadic methods are a(n):

_____ Optimal match

_____ Acceptable match

_____ Poor match or not a match

Sources: Adapted from Sharan, Y., & Sharan, S. (1992). Expanding cooperative learning through group investigation. New York: Teachers College Press; Slavin, R. E. (1991). Synthesis of research of cooperative learning. Educational Leadership, 48(5), 71–82; Slavin, R. E. (1995). Cooperative learning: Theory, research, and practice (2nd ed.). Needham Heights, MA: Allyn & Bacon.

Cooperative Learning Student Self-Assessment Rubric

Team # _____ Team Member _____

3 As a Team We:	2 As a Team We:	1 As a Team We:
☐ Consistently and actively worked toward group goals	☐ Worked toward group goals with occasional prompting	☐ Worked toward group goals only when prompted
☐ Cared about each other's successes in learning as much as our own	☐ Somewhat understood that the team's success is dependent on each of us being successful	☐ Cared only about individual learning
☐ Continuously interacted with each other, providing constructive input, supporting and encouraging each other, and solving problems efficiently	☐ Interacted with each other positively to a certain degree	☐ Did not have the rapport and trust to work cooperatively
3 As a Team Member I:	2 As a Team Member I:	1 As a Team Member I:
☐ Continuously supported and encouraged the others	☐ Offered help only when I was asked	☐ Did not help my team members at all
☐ Stayed open-minded and listened to my team members' ideas	☐ Tried to listen to others' ideas but was not patient	☐ Did not listen to my team members' ideas
☐ Routinely provided useful ideas and showed strong effort	☐ Sometimes provided useful ideas and satisfactorily did what was required	☐ Rarely provided useful ideas and did not contribute

Sources: Adapted from Johnson, D. W., & Johnson, R. T. (1999a). Learning together and alone: Cooperative, competitive, and individualistic learning *(5th ed.).* Boston: Allyn & Bacon; Johnson, D. W., & Johnson, R. T. (1999b). *Making cooperative learning work.* Theory Into Practice, 38(2), 67–73.

Cooperative Learning Teacher Reflection

The following questions help teachers reflect on the use of cooperative learning.

Positive Interdependence

- How well did the groups meet the learning goals?
- Were the rewards (for individuals or groups) fair? Did they encourage students to work as a team and commit to their learning both as an individual and as a team?
- How did the role assignment of the team members work?
- Did I distribute the resources in such a way that students had to share resources with the group as a whole in order to succeed?
- Were the learning tasks designed in a way optimal for student cooperation? Did the product require contributions from each member?

Individual and Group Accountability

- Was each student individually held accountable for knowing the information and doing his or her share of the work?
- Did I check for individual accountability, such as by posing a question or a problem and randomly calling on specific individuals to give an explanation after talking about the question or problem in a group?
- What opportunities did I put in place for individual team members to demonstrate the knowledge and skills that the team was assigned to learn?

Promotive Interaction

- What was the quality of ongoing interactions among the students?
- Did the students engage in ongoing conversation, exchange, and support throughout the learning activity?
- Did I explain the interaction behaviors I expect to observe during the lesson?
- What feedback did I provide when students demonstrated undesired behaviors?

Interpersonal and Small-Group Skills

- Did students learn specific social skills because of this cooperative learning experience?
- How did the students do in terms of expressing their ideas, appreciating different perspectives, group decision making, group problem solving, and conflict resolution?

Instructional Strategies for Effective Teaching © 2016 Solution Tree Press • solution-tree.com
Visit **go.solution-tree.com/instruction** to download this page.

Group Processing

- Did I provide the students with opportunities to evaluate and discuss the effectiveness of their learning experience?

- Did I provide the students opportunities to generate ideas or suggestions for future improvement?

- Did I have students celebrate the success of work done as a team?

Sources: Adapted from Johnson, D. W., & Johnson, R. T. (1999a). Learning together and alone: Cooperative, competitive, and individualistic learning *(5th ed.). Boston: Allyn & Bacon; Johnson, D. W., & Johnson, R. T. (1999b). Making cooperative learning work.* Theory Into Practice, *38(2), 67–73.*

Chapter 5
Direct Instruction

Direct instruction isn't glamorous. As the name implies, educators often construe it as a no-frills, teacher-directed approach to instruction. Since the 1970s, teachers have continued to view it—and use it—as a viable teaching tool, largely because it gets student achievement results. Maybe the approach is not glamorous —but the results are.

Direct instruction does *not* mean all lecture or "drill and kill." Prominent features of direct instruction include (Joyce et al., 2004):

- A focus on academic tasks and learning

- A high degree of teacher direction and control of the learning process

- High expectations for student progress

- A learning environment in which every minute counts

- A relatively neutral atmosphere marked by avoidance of negative practices such as criticism

In general terms, direct instruction is an instructional method in which the teacher explains a new concept or skill to students in a large-group setting, has the students test their understanding through practice under the teacher's direction, and then continues with guided practice (Joyce et al., 2004).

What Research Says About Direct Instruction

Direct instruction is one of the most, if not *the* most, researched instructional approaches. Siegfried Engelmann and his colleagues created this model in the 1960s at the University of Illinois at Urbana-Champaign under the Project Follow Through grant. Between 1968 and 1978, Engelmann and his team conducted one of the largest longitudinal studies ever completed concerning instructional practices. The study involved approximately 75,000 students at 180 sites and compared direct instruction with twelve other instructional models (as cited in Kame'enui, Simmons, Chard, & Dickson, 1997). They found that the direct instruction approach produces greater gains in a variety of outcomes measures—including basic skills, cognitive problem solving, engagement, and student affect (self-esteem)—than other educational models (Kame'enui et al., 1997). More specifically, consider the following research findings.

- Students who receive instructional treatments that incorporate direct instruction perform significantly better at identifying the main idea while reading than students who receive no such treatments (Stevens, Slavin, & Farnish, 1991).

- Low-achieving students who receive basic multiplication lessons with explicit instruction perform significantly better than peers taught with a constructivist approach and those in the control group (Kroesbergen, Van Luit, & Maas, 2004).

- Direct instruction is a more effective and efficient approach to teaching phonological awareness skills to preschool students with language delays than an activity-based intervention that is student initiated (Botts, Losardo, Tillery, & Werts, 2014).

- Teachers have used direct instruction effectively in both general and special education classrooms (Algozzine & Maheady, 1986; Ledford, Lane, Elam, & Wolery, 2012).

- Elementary science students who receive direct instruction as compared to connected instruction (instruction that explicitly connects current learning with prior knowledge) demonstrate greater achievement gains in the short term but have a higher rate of loss of science knowledge over time (Upadhyay & DeFranco, 2008).

Teachers do not have to implement direct instruction alone; they can integrate it with other instructional media, such as technology, and other instructional approaches, such as inquiry-based learning. One study finds that integrating technology with direct instruction can improve student learning in mathematics by 23 percent (Al-Shammari, Aqeel, Faulkner, & Ansari, 2012). Another study indicates that a balanced combination of direct instruction and inquiry-based instruction leads to greater improvement in student critical thinking (Ku, Ho, Hau, & Lai, 2014); this study's version of direct instruction includes PowerPoint slides with clear learning objectives, step-by-step explanations for carrying out critical thinking (which include explicit instruction emphasizing why, when, where, and how to use the skill), and examples of discrete critical-thinking skills.

How to Move From Research to Practice

It is worth mentioning again that direct instruction is not a lecture approach; instead, it is an instructional method that focuses on the interaction between teachers and students around subject matter (Magliaro, Lockee, & Burton, 2005). The basis of direct instruction is a systematic process focused on observing and modeling to influence behavior. This process includes the following practices (Preast, 2009).

- **Orientation:** The teacher clarifies the learning task and student expectations.

- **Presentation:** The teacher explains and demonstrates a new task.

- **Structured practice:** The teacher uses examples to guide statements in learning a new task.

- **Guided practice:** Students practice with the teacher's help.

- **Independent practice:** Students practice until they have mastered the task.

Joyce et al. (2004) recommend short, intense, highly motivated practice periods. For example, with younger students, short, five- to ten-minute practice sessions interspersed throughout the day are more effective than long, thirty- to forty-minute sessions.

There are numerous models and applications of direct instruction that have proven successful and gained widespread acceptance in education, ranging from general to special education, from elementary to high school (and beyond), and from basic skill attainment to critical-thinking skills. For the sake of brevity (and hopefully clarity), we have chosen to highlight three models in table 5.1 that have gained popularity over the years—(1) Barak Rosenshine's (1985) Explicit Teaching Model, (2) Madeline Hunter's (1976, 1982) Design of Effective Lessons Model, and (3) Robert Gagné's (1985) Events of Instruction Model—using a three-stage approach originally developed by Carl Bereiter and Siegfried Engelmann (1966).

Direct instruction is a straightforward form of teaching. It helps teachers tackle well-defined content using systematic and chronological instruction based on scripted lesson plans. Direct instruction often features fast-paced and efficient teacher-student interactions. One of Engelmann's slogans is "If the student hasn't learned, the teacher hasn't taught." He founded direct instruction on the belief that student learning is not an accidental occurrence but a result of deliberate and careful design of progressive small steps based on learning theory.

Summary

Direct instruction is an approach that focuses on making implicit understanding explicit and available for immediate use. It aims to help students understand not only the importance of certain knowledge or skills but also how and why they work. Compared with inquiry-based learning, which will be introduced later in this book, direct instruction is more directive and structured. For pedagogical best results, we recommend that teachers not rely on a single format of teaching but instead combine the approaches from both ends of the scale of directiveness in order to enhance student learning.

Table 5.1: Direct Instruction Models

Stage	Rosenshine's (1985) Explicit Teaching Model	Hunter's (1976, 1982) Design of Effective Lessons Model	Gagné's (1985) Events of Instruction Model
1. Introduction	Review: • Evaluate and review homework. • Assess and review relevant previous learning. • Explain the connections between prerequisite skills and knowledge for this lesson.	• Encourage students to focus. • Gather student diagnostic information related to the lesson. • Introduce objective and purpose of the lesson.	• Gain student attention. • Inform students of learning objectives.
2. Main lesson presentation	Presentation: • State lesson objectives. • Provide outline. • Teach in small steps. • Model procedures. • Provide examples. • Check for understanding.	• Conduct task analysis to determine what knowledge and skills students need to learn. • Use pedagogical strategies appropriate for the lesson. • Demonstrate the model.	• Stimulate recall of prerequisite learning. • Present instructional material. • Provide learning guidance.
3. Practice	Practice: • Offer guided practice. • Present correction and feedback. • Offer independent practice. • Hold periodic reviews (weekly, monthly).	• Check for understanding. • Offer guided practice. • Offer independent practice.	• Practice. • Provide feedback and focus on correctness of performance. • Assess performance. • Enhance retention and transfer of learning.

Source: Adapted from the cross-walk analysis of Magliaro et al., 2005.

Direct instruction is helpful for teaching critical content of the subject matter—the skills, strategies, vocabulary terms, concepts, and rules. There are many models of direct instruction, but they all typically involve three major steps: (1) introduction, (2) presentation, and (3) practice. We present these steps as three interconnected handouts that capture the major characteristics of direct instruction. Teachers can use these handouts to design lessons that ensure (or, at the very least, enhance the likelihood of) student success in learning.

The first handout, "How to Deliver an Effective Introduction" (page 52), is about how to introduce effective instruction for a lesson using direct instruction. David Sousa (2011) explains that during a learning episode, students tend to remember best what is taught first, second best what is taught last, and least what is taught in the middle. This is known as the primacy-recency effect. It indicates that the beginning of a lesson matters in terms of how to make the most of classroom time.

Teachers should conduct presentations in direct instruction in a clear and organized manner. The handout "How to Deliver an Effective Presentation" (page 53) guides instructional delivery.

In direct instruction, the practice component typically occurs in a sequence of controlled or guided practice followed by free or independent practice. The handout "How to Develop Effective Practice Activities" (page 54) can assist teachers in thinking through the practice process as they transition from supervision and guidance to less-scaffolded activities.

How to Deliver an Effective Introduction

Start the lesson with a review of previously learned skills, homework, or prerequisites students will need to accomplish the target lesson. The review will informally assess students so you can gauge whether they are ready for the new learning or if reteaching is necessary prior to the delivery of the new lesson.

List what you will review and how you will review it prior to the target lesson.

- Homework?
- Questioning so that students can recall previous learning?
- Prerequisite knowledge and skills needed for the new learning?

Then provide an overview of the lesson, such as by verbally stating or listing the learning objectives.

- Identify the goals for the lesson.
- Provide an outline of the lesson.

Reflections:

How to Deliver an Effective Presentation

Teach the new knowledge or skills at a fast pace to maintain student attention and in small increments to ensure student understanding.

1. Identify the major steps you will use for the explanation:

2. Identify the key points you will use in your explanations of the new learning:

3. Good exemplars and non-exemplars play an important role in explanations. Identify the exemplars and non-exemplars you will use:

4. Model the procedures, such as thinking aloud, and use clear and consistent language.

   Describe how you will model the new learning:

5. Monitor student understanding by asking questions and providing modified explanations or demonstrations as needed.

   Identify the major questions you will use to gauge student understanding:

   Identify the alternative explanations or demonstrations you can use if the initial ones are insufficient:

6. Record any reflections:

How to Develop Effective Practice Activities

For guided practice, advise students of the strategies and resources available to scaffold them in learning content. Continue guided practice until students can answer approximately 80 percent of the questions correctly.

Consider the instructional support you will provide, such as cues, hints, or prompts:

For free practice, help students internalize new skills and knowledge by engaging in more autonomous learning activities.

Design learning activities that parallel the guided practice but with the support removed:

Identify the strategies you will use to deepen student learning and integration of new knowledge, such as asking students to provide details or more complexity:

Provide feedback based on students' performance to assess and facilitate learning. Keep in mind that feedback timing is important in direct instruction. You should give immediate feedback on student misconceptions or faulty interpretations. Consider your feedback along with the four feedback categories identified by John Hattie and Helen Timperley (2007). Each of these types of feedback impacts student learning differently, with the two middle categories proving most effective.

1. **Feedback about the task (recommended):** How well a task is being accomplished or performed, such as distinguishing correct from incorrect answers

2. **Feedback about the processing of the task (highly recommended):** The specific cognitive processes that underlie tasks, such as information regarding the relationship between strategies taken and quality of performance

3. **Feedback about self-regulation (highly recommended):** The way students monitor, direct, and regulate actions toward the learning goal

4. **Feedback about the self as a person (not recommended):** A personal evaluation of the students, such as "great effort"

Reflections:

Source: Adapted from Hattie, J., & Timperley, H. (2007). The power of feedback. Review of Educational Research, *77(1), 81–112.*

Chapter 6
Mastery Learning

Anyone who has taught knows that students learn in different ways and at different rates. One well-tested approach for addressing students' unique learning needs is mastery learning—an instructional method that gives a detailed and personalized roadmap of expectations for each student. The basic features of mastery learning are:

- Preassessing student learning
- Developing appropriate learning objectives
- Providing individualized learning experiences
- Postassessing student learning progress
- Moving on if students achieve mastery
- Providing further instruction or learning experiences to attain mastery

In essence, this is a test-before-you-teach approach to designing and guiding instruction. In mastery learning, students continuously receive corrective feedback and advice for improvement from the teacher regarding their specified tasks. Also, teachers expect students to remain conscious of their present positions, their upcoming goals, and the ways they can bridge the gap between the two. In this manner, mastery learning takes student learning differences into account—their prior achievements, learning styles, and learning paces—and then sets individualized, specific, and sequential learning goals.

Most teachers are familiar with the instructional approach of mastery learning, especially with the contemporary focus on achieving mastery on state- or district-mandated curriculum goals. In a mastery learning classroom, the assessment approach is formative and individual-referenced, rather than criteria-referenced or norm-referenced like many other assessments. Additionally, the teacher avoids rote memory methods or superficial learning merely for the purpose of pushing

students to a passing score on a high-stakes test. Mastery learning has many advantages; it:

- Ensures students have the prerequisite knowledge and skills before they move on with their learning
- Offers alternative learning opportunities, builds students' success with learning, and breaks the cycle of failure
- Makes teachers more knowledgeable about the status of student learning, and guides and adjusts planning based on students' needs
- Sets high expectations with meaningful learning objectives that every student can master

We attribute the application of mastery learning in education to, among others, Benjamin Bloom (1984). Although behaviorist learning models—such as mastery learning—tend to recall the stimulus-response conditioning experiments conducted by Ivan Pavlov and others, mastery learning is far from mechanistic. A key advantage of mastery learning, as compared with some cognitive models, is that it not only targets the content domain but also takes into account student readiness when targeting learning objectives. Additionally, teachers can use it to design and implement instruction that focuses on the student as an individual—another key advantage in a results-oriented environment.

What Research Says About Mastery Learning

In Bloom's (1984) seminal study, students taught with a mastery learning approach score approximately one standard deviation above the average student taught by traditional methods. In other words, mastery learning students' achievement is at the 84th percentile while students in the traditional classroom are at the 50th percentile. Bloom's (1984) findings also suggest that mastery learning can be an effective tool for decreasing learning gaps among students. He notes that achievement differences between faster and slower learners should decrease with successive units of mastery learning, leading to smaller variance among students. A well-known proposition from Bloom states that 90 percent of students can learn required content if they are given appropriate instruction and enough time. *Appropriate instruction* means teachers compartmentalize the learning into units of learning and require students to demonstrate mastery of specified objectives for one unit before they move on to the next unit. *Enough time* refers to the amount of engaged learning time students need to demonstrate mastery of objectives.

In addition, mastery learning has a positive effect on students' retention of the material they learn, increases time on task, improves their attendance, and lowers course attrition rates (Guskey & Pigott, 1988). Of forty-three mastery learning studies reviewed by Thomas Guskey and Therese Pigott (1988), almost all of them show positive effects on student achievement, with effect sizes ranging from 0.02 to 1.70. More specifically, average effect sizes were 0.50 for science, 0.53 for social studies, 0.60 for language arts, and 0.70 for mathematics. Additionally, average effect sizes were 0.94 for students in first grade through eighth grade, and 0.48 for high school students (Guskey & Pigott, 1988).

Johnson Changeiywo, P. W. Wambugu, and S. W. Wachanga (2011) find that students taught using mastery learning have higher motivation to learn the subject matter than those taught with regular teaching methods. Students are motivated because mastering small instructional objectives can help build confidence as they proceed to the next unit. Also, in the process of mastery learning, teachers often give corrective feedback immediately to enable students to know their areas of weakness and work on them (Changeiywo et al., 2011). An interesting point to note is that while mastery learning has been researched extensively since the mid-1990s in the K–12 setting, researchers now use and study it widely at the higher education level (Diegelman-Parente, 2011; Roberts, Ingram, Flack, & Hayes, 2013).

How to Move From Research to Practice

In mastery learning, the teacher identifies learning objectives on a step-by-step, student-by-student basis. It works particularly well with hierarchically and sequentially ordered subjects, such as mathematics and science. The following three steps, adapted from James Block and Robert Burns (1976) and Thomas Guskey (2010), delineate the major aspects of mastery learning.

Step 1 is defining mastery. A teacher needs to define *mastery* of the subject. This involves the actions to:

- Clearly define what teachers expect all students to learn by formulating a set of objectives

- Prepare a final or summative assessment covering these objectives and determine what level of mastery teachers expect all students to achieve

- Break the learning into a sequence of smaller units

- Determine the objectives teachers will cover in each unit

Step 2 is planning for mastery. Once teachers have defined the goal of mastery, they must plan instructional procedures to help each student master the objectives in each unit. These plans may include how to initially present each unit's material, involving students in the learning, and developing feedback and correction procedures (such as brief, diagnostic progress reviews or formative assessments) teachers can use at the close of each unit's initial instruction. These assessments provide information on each student's learning as a result of the unit's initial instruction. A teacher needs to specify a score or performance standard on this test, typically 80 to 90 percent correct, which, when met, indicates unit mastery. Step 2 also involves developing a set of alternative instructional materials and procedures—or corrective learning activities—keyed to each item on the unit's formative test. Teachers design these corrective activities to reteach the material tested by each item but in ways that differ from the unit's initial instruction.

The final step is implementing the plan. During the implementation phase, the teacher delivers the learning units in sequence using planned initial instructional methods. When teachers employ an approach that allows students to learn at their own pace, they can move through the course or unit as quickly as practical or as slowly as needed.

After the teacher has completed the instruction for a given learning unit, and before moving to the next unit, he or she administers the unit's formative tests. Using the test results, the teacher identifies those students who have achieved the unit mastery standard and those who have not. The assessment data should be used as part of the teaching and learning process to provide individualized feedback about student learning and then to prescribe specific remediation or support activities. The mastery students are free to engage in enrichment and extension activities or to serve as tutors for their nonmastery classmates. For the students who have not acquired the expected competency, the teacher provides appropriate corrective or revised learning opportunities to complete their unit learning. The slowest 5 percent of learners need an estimated five times as much time to reach mastery as do the fastest 5 percent of learners (Bloom, 1984). In many cases, mastery learning incorporates strategies that require changing the pace of instruction. However, that is not always necessary. Teachers can also schedule alternative or revised learning outside of the classroom. Typically, corrective activities should take about 10 to 20 percent of the time of the initial instruction. For example, for a week-long unit, the corrective activities should take about one day.

Teachers can repeat this cycle of initial instruction, student progress tracking, and certification or alternative and remedial learning unit by unit until they have taught all units and the students have mastered each one. At the end, teachers administer the final or summative examination to assess the success of student learning.

Summary

Mastery learning is an instructional strategy that uses formative assessment and corrective procedures so that all students can master the established level of performance. High-quality feedback and sufficient learning opportunities are crucial to the success of student learning, according to mastery learning. It is also based on the belief that intelligence and aptitude are not the most prominent predictor of student learning; instead, enough time and appropriate learning conditions are the keys for all students to achieve the expected level of learning.

The core of mastery learning is to accommodate the diversity of student learning and to ensure the success of learning for *all* students. This approach is most beneficial for linear or sequential subject matter; preferably, teachers divide it into units with specified objectives. In this way, it's easier for students to demonstrate mastery on unit exams before moving to a new unit. Students who do not demonstrate mastery then receive remedial or supportive learning from the teacher along with more time. The "Mastery Learning Unit" handout (page 58) will help teachers plan a unit on mastery learning.

Tracking student progress is a key component of mastery learning. The process should empower students and teachers to analyze strengths and growth areas and bridge the gap to the predetermined goals. The handout "Tracking Student Progress" (page 59) can help teachers track each student's progress after each assessment, organize student data, and see trends in student learning to identify what types of teaching practices are working best for the students. For students in higher grade levels, teachers can hand out the chart and ask them to calculate and record their own mastery. The students should receive a new chart for each new unit. Note that assessment 2 should parallel assessment 1; teachers should administer it after nonmastery students have received the corrective instruction.

We have designed the handout "Mastery Chart" (page 61) to assist teachers or students by providing an at-a-glance summary of the learning status of the whole class. The teacher can post this on the wall and use different colored sticky notes to mark each level of progress toward mastery. The process of teaching the unit should allow for the shapes to change as students move closer to the mastery goal. At the end of the unit, a majority of the students should demonstrate mastery before moving on with the next unit, and those who have yet to achieve mastery receive more time and help.

Mastery Learning Unit

The learning objectives of this unit are:

The definition of mastery for this unit is:

I have planned enough materials for initial instruction. These materials include:

I have planned materials for the corrective or supportive instruction for nonmastery students and the enrichment instruction for mastery students. These materials include:

The approach for alternative learning includes:

☐ Tutoring

☐ Peer tutoring

☐ Small-group discussion

☐ Additional homework

☐ Other _____

I have a variety of parallel tests for assessing and reassessing, which include:

The final assessment indicates _____ percent of students have demonstrated mastery.

Goal accomplished?

☐ Yes

☐ No

Tracking Student Progress

Unit 1: _____

100%												
90%												
80%												
70%												
60%												
50%												

Instructional Strategies for Effective Teaching © 2016 J. H. Stronge • solution-tree.com

Visit **go.solution-tree.com/instruction** to download this page.

	Assessment 1	Assessment 2	End-of-Unit Test	Assessment 1	Assessment 2	End-of-Unit Test	Assessment 1	Assessment 2	End-of-Unit Test	Assessment 1	Assessment 2	End-of-Unit Test
Learning Objectives	Learning Objective 1:			Learning Objective 2:			Learning Objective 3:			Learning Objective 4:		
Percent Mastery												
10%												
20%												
30%												
40%												

Reflections:

Mastery Chart

What Have You Mastered? (80% or above)

	Unit 1				Unit 2				Unit 3			
	Learning Objective 1	Learning Objective 2	Learning Objective 3	Learning Objective 4	Learning Objective 1	Learning Objective 2	Learning Objective 3	Learning Objective 4	Learning Objective 1	Learning Objective 2	Learning Objective 3	Learning Objective 4
Student 1												
Student 2												
Student 3												
Student 4												
Student 5												
Student 6												
Student 7												
Student 8												
Student 9												
Student 10												
Student 11												
Student 12												
Student 13												
Student 14												
Student 15												

Key:

△ = Falls Far Behind   ◯ = Meets

☐ = Approaches   ☆ = Exceeds

Instructional Strategies for Effective Teaching © 2016 J. H. Stronge • solution-tree.com

Visit **go.solution-tree.com/instruction** to download this page.

Chapter 7
Memorization and Mnemonic Instruction

People think of human memory as a continuously active system that receives, encodes, modifies, stores, and retrieves information. Although memory, perceptions, learning, and problem solving are distinct functions of our brains, they overlap and are closely related. When we analyze in detail what occurs in the mental processes of perception, learning, thinking, and remembering, it becomes clear that many cognitive functions are common to these operations.

By *memorization*, we do not mean rote procedures that involve going over new information until it is implanted in the memory. Rote memory means fixing information in the brain through sheer repetition. In this method, we intend memorization to include an elaborate teaching and learning strategy that helps learners master content more quickly and retain it longer. Memorization and recitation of poetry, for instance, are an important part of the reading process: they exercise the student's memory, help the student mentally store beautiful language, and give the student practice in speaking aloud (Bauer & Wise, 2009). Within the context of this broader definition of memorization, we focus on *mnemonic instruction* as a tool for increasing long-term memory recall and use of knowledge.

Memorization and mnemonic instruction are great techniques for processing and storing information. For instance, one can convert the word *occipital* (the region of the brain that controls vision) to *exhibit hall* because they are acoustically alike. The students can visualize walking into an art museum and seeing a painting of a brain with a big, bulging eye (Thorne, 2006). A quick and accurate memory aids not only recall but also many learning processes. As such, memorization is a highly valuable instructional approach that can help students develop cues when storing and retrieving information.

What Research Says About Memorization

According to Thomas Scruggs and Margo Mastropieri (2000), "one of the most commonly described problems of students with learning and behavioral difficulties is memory for academic content" (p. 163). In their 2000 study, Scruggs and Mastropieri examine the effects of mnemonic (memory-enhancing) strategies in addressing this critical area of need. They synthesize thirty-four experiments reported in twenty-nine journal articles and find that mnemonic techniques have a mean effect size of 1.62 (a difference of 45 percentile points), indicating an unusually large treatment effect. In another study, Scruggs and Mastropieri (1991) evaluate the effectiveness of mnemonic instruction of science content in the classroom for nineteen students with mild disabilities. The research suggests that mnemonic instruction results in substantial increases in initial content acquisition and substantially higher delayed-recall scores over more traditional instructional procedures. Furthermore, the study finds that trained students are able to successfully generate and apply their own mnemonic strategies to new content. Also, students overwhelmingly prefer mnemonic instruction over traditional instructional methods. In another study, middle school students who read several passages about the accomplishments of famous people remembered more names and accomplishment information when they used mnemonic imagery than those who did not (Peters & Levin, 1986). The study finds that mnemonic instruction is beneficial for both above- and below-average readers on short fictional passages, as well as on longer nonfictional passages taken from actual school reading materials.

Mnemonic strategy has been widely used and researched in language learning, especially in second language learning and vocabulary acquisition. The findings overwhelmingly favor mnemonic instruction (Amiryousefi & Ketabi, 2011; Khoii & Sharififar, 2013), which involves "a specific reconstruction of target content intended to tie new information more closely to the learner's existing knowledge base and, therefore, facilitate retrieval" (Scruggs & Mastropieri, 1990, p. 272). A study by Michael Dunn (2011) indicates that mnemonic instruction can help students improve writing skills. It finds that mnemonic strategy offers a means to better organize the thinking process to accomplish a task.

Jennie Grammer, Jennifer Coffman, and Peter Ornstein (2013) also find when students receive memory-rich science instruction—that is, when teachers use more memory-relevant language to help students adopt a method or procedure for remembering information, such as, "If you are having trouble thinking of ways to connect the wheel and axle, you can look at the diagram to help you"—they exhibit greater levels of strategic knowledge and engage in more sophisticated strategy use in memory tasks than students exposed to low-memory instruction. Joyce et al. (2004) suggest that the effects of memory instruction could be threefold.

1. Increase students' awareness of how to learn and improve learning results.

2. Improve students' capacity for imagination and generate the realization that creative forms of thinking are an essential part of convergent, information-oriented learning.

3. Strengthen students' capacity for remembering materials.

In summary, memorization and mnemonic instruction provide a well-researched set of strategies that enhance student learning and can readily be woven into a wide range of other instructional strategies.

How to Move From Research to Practice

Although teachers want students to develop higher-order thinking skills, factual knowledge still matters. In many circumstances, higher-order thinking starts with a solid foundation of knowledge. To learn chemistry, for instance, students must study the names and abbreviations of elements, along with their structural properties. Factual knowledge is often a prerequisite for more advanced work in a discipline, yet in the classroom, teachers often present content to students in a short timeframe. Consequently, only the content provided with added attention enters the memory. Furthermore, receptive knowledge is distinct from productive knowledge. Students need to practice or rehearse content retrieval frequently enough to establish it for the long term. Joyce et al. (2004) propose a four-step model with goals to both teach memorization and help students learn more effectively.

1. Direct students' attention to new material. Use techniques like underlining, listing, and reflecting to allow students to attend to and be aware of the new information.

2. Develop connections between unfamiliar and familiar material by using keyword, substitute-word, and link-system techniques. The purpose of such associations is to provide a richer mental context; these additional keywords, substitute words, and links provide anchors within the information-processing procedures.

   - The keyword technique means one word represents a longer thought or several subordinate thoughts.

   - The substitute-word technique makes an intangible concept tangible and meaningful.

   - The link-system technique generates associations of two ideas.

3. Use interesting techniques such as exaggeration, ridiculous association, and out-of-proportion rules (like making small things gigantic or large things miniature) to make the association more vivid or dramatic so students can better retain it.

4. Practice recalling the material until students have completely learned it.

A cooperative classroom climate facilitates these specific memory techniques. The teacher and students should become a team working on the new material together. At the initial stage, the teacher can more explicitly teach the strategy. The teacher helps students identify key learning objects, keywords, and associations, and offers suggestions as needed. When students are familiar with the strategy, they increasingly master it and use it independently to memorize ideas, words, and formulas (Joyce et al., 2004).

Another memory technique is the use of pegwords, which are rhyming proxies for numbers—one is *bun*, two is *shoe*, three is *tree*, and so on—and are effective for remembering numbered or ordered information. For instance, as noted by Scruggs and Mastropieri (2000),

> To remember that insects have six legs, a picture can be drawn of insects on sticks. A picture of spiders on a gate (pegword for 8) can help students remember that spiders have eight legs. Likewise, a jury of *elves* (*elf* is the pegword for 12) can help students remember that juries have 12 members (Mastropieri & Scruggs, 1991).

> Pegwords also can be combined with keywords. For example, to remember that Monroe was the fifth president, students can be shown a picture of *money* (keyword for Monroe) being carried by bees to a *hive* (pegword for 5; Mastropieri, Scruggs, & Whedon, 1997). To remember that the mineral crocoite is number 2 on the Mohs hardness scale, students can be shown a picture of *crocodiles* (keyword for crocoite) wearing *shoes* (pegword for 2). (pp. 164–165)

Educators have developed a variety of similar techniques under the category of mnemonic instruction, with the most significant being keywords. An example of mnemonic instruction may help illuminate how it can work within a classroom:

> To teach that *vituperation* is a word designating abusive speech, learners first are taught a keyword for the unfamiliar term, vituperation. In this case, viper is a good keyword for vituperation, because it is acoustically similar to vituperation, and can be pictured. The resulting mnemonic picture would depict a viper speaking abusively to someone, therefore effectively integrating the pictured concept with the keyword. When asked to retrieve the definition of "vituperation," then, learners are asked to first think of the keyword, viper, think back to the picture with the viper in it, and think of what was happening in the picture to retrieve the information, "abusive speech." Thus, mnemonic instruction improves recall by systematically integrating specific retrieval routes within to-be-learned content. (Scruggs & Mastropieri, 1990, p. 273)

Dunn (2011) uses acronyms as a mnemonic memory technique. For instance, one teacher used the SCOTTISH mnemonic to provide a sequential process for students to manage each step in creating the desired writing product:

> **S**elect an idea, problem, or solution.
>
> **C**reate the scenario.
>
> **O**rganize the problems and possible solutions.
>
> **T**alk about the story starter; create a mental picture to help generate ideas.
>
> **T**ype responses.
>
> **I**nclude step-by-step directions to help manage writing tasks.
>
> **S**tart a new subtopic (for the storyline "a trip to Mars," students could first write about what they know of Mars; then they could describe what they think living on Mars would be like).
>
> **H**ave fun with it; make the storyline writing tasks interesting for students. (p. 21)

There are a number of commercially available publications on mnemonic tools. For example, *Vocabulary Cartoons: SAT Word Power* (Burchers, Burchers, & Burchers, 2013) is a collection of rhyming words and visual mnemonic aids for rapid enhancement in learning SAT vocabulary.

Summary

Learning and memory are closely connected concepts. Memory depends on and is initiated by learning. It records the knowledge or skill acquired through learning processes. On the other hand, learning also depends on memory because the knowledge and past behavior stored in memory provide a framework to link new knowledge and skill. Memorization and mnemonic strategies are instructional techniques that help students encode, retain, and retrieve information.

As noted, the keyword method is one of the most versatile mnemonic strategies and is helpful whenever students must remember new vocabulary or names for new facts and concepts (Scruggs & Mastropieri, 2000). Teachers can use the handout "Mnemonic Strategies" with students to teach them how to use this mnemonic technique. The teacher can model and offer assistance initially, and students can use the diagram to create their own lists of words to learn. The handout is also useful to help students create pegwords for numbers, keywords, or anything else. There are many versions of pegwords available. With this handout, the teacher can pick those that are most appropriate and even develop unique ones with the students; this practice encourages ownership of learning.

Letter strategies include acronyms, acrostics (a composition in which certain letters in each line form a word or words), and summarized lists of information. The handout "Letter Strategies" (page 68) provides examples from a variety of subject areas. Teachers can also combine letter strategies with the keyword strategy. For example, to help students remember that the countries of the Central Powers were Turkey, Austria-Hungary, and Germany, teachers can show students a picture of children playing *TAG* (acronym for Turkey, Austria-Hungary, and Germany) in *Central Park* (keyword for Central Powers) (Scruggs & Mastropieri, 2000).

Mnemonic Strategies

Following are two methods to incorporate mnemonics into instruction.

Keyword Method

New word to learn:

- *Peavey* (hook)

Recode the word into a keyword that is concrete (easy to picture), already familiar, and acoustically similar.

- Pea

Make the connection between them.

- Imagining a picture where a pea is hung on a hook

Pegword Method

 One is a bun.

 Seven is heaven.

 Two is a shoe.

 Eight is a gate.

 Three is a tree.

 Nine is a line.

 Four is a door.

 Ten is a hen.

 Five is a hive.

 Eleven is a lever.

 Six is a pile of sticks.

 Twelve is an elf.

Letter Strategies

Strategy	Information to Memorize
Science	
My Very Easy Method Just Speeds Up Naming Planets My Very Excited Mother Just Served Us Nine Pies My Very Educated Mother Just Served Us Noodles (without Pluto)	The planets in order: Mercury, Venus, Earth, Mars, Jupiter, Saturn, Uranus, Neptune, Pluto
Roy G. Biv	The colors of the rainbow: red, orange, yellow, green, blue, indigo, violet
Kids Prefer Cheese Over Fried Green Spinach	The order of taxonomy: kingdom, phylum, class, order, family, genus, species
Pvt. Tim Hall	Essential amino acids: phenylalanine, valine, threonine, tryptophan, isoleucine, methionine, histidine, arginine, leucine, lysine
Mathematics	
Dear Miss Sally Brown	The main steps in long division: divide, multiply, subtract, bring down
Please Excuse My Dear Aunt Sally	Order of mathematics operations: parentheses, exponents, multiply, divide, add, and subtract
Geography	
Super Man Helps Every One	The order of the Great Lakes from west to east: Superior, Michigan, Huron, Erie, Ontario
History and Social Studies	
Will A Jolly Man Make A Jolly Visitor?	The first eight U.S. presidents: George Washington, John Adams, Thomas Jefferson, James Madison, James Monroe, John Quincy Adams, Andrew Jackson, Martin Van Buren
Large Elephants Jump Slowly And Sink Rapidly	The seven articles of the U.S. Constitution: legislative, executive, judicial, supremacy, amendment, statehood, ratification

Source: Adapted from Mnemonic Devices Memory Tools. (n.d.). What is a mnemonic device? *Accessed at www.mnemonic-device .com/what-is-a-mnemonic-device on February 18, 2015.*

Instructional Strategies for Effective Teaching © 2016 Solution Tree Press • solution-tree.com

Visit **go.solution-tree.com/instruction** to download this page.

Chapter 8

Inquiry-Based Learning

Inquiry-based learning as an instructional method is a student-centered, active learning approach focused on questioning, critical thinking, and problem solving. There are many definitions of inquiry-based learning. The National Research Council (NRC, 2000) defines inquiry as a

> multifaceted activity that involves making observations; posing questions; examining books and other sources of information to see what is already known; planning investigations; reviewing what is already known in light of experimental evidence; using tools to gather, analyze, and interpret data; proposing answers, explanations, and predictions; and communicating the results. Inquiry requires identification of assumptions, use of critical and logical thinking, and consideration of alternative explanations. (p. 23)

Similarly, Hattie (2009) describes inquiry as an instructional approach in which the teacher develops challenging situations for students to:

- Observe and question phenomena
- Pose explanations of what they observe
- Devise and conduct experiments in which data are collected to support or contradict their theories
- Analyze data related to their theories
- Draw conclusions from experimental data
- Design and build models based on the findings

He writes,

> Such learning situations are meant to be open-ended in that they do not aim to achieve a single "right" answer for a particular question being addressed, but rather involve students more in the process of observing, posing questions, engaging in experimentation or exploration, and learning to analyze and reason. (Hattie, 2009, pp. 208–209)

Inquiry-based learning is a great way for students to practice the scientific method on authentic questions (Savery, 2006); some go so far as to say that one can't consider certain hands-on activities, such as examining and tracing fossils, to be inquiry-based learning if teachers conduct them in the absence of research questions (Bunterm et al., 2014). As such, inquiry-based learning is used most commonly in areas of science, such as physics, chemistry, and biology. This chapter explores how teachers of a wide range of grades can use inquiry-based learning to more effectively teach investigation skills to students through the application of a scientific method approach.

What Research Says About Inquiry-Based Learning

Inquiry-based learning is one of the most studied instructional approaches, and research findings generally favor it. A research synthesis by Daphne Minner, Abigail Levy, and Jeanne Century (2010) reviews 138 studies of inquiry-based learning and finds that just over half of the studies show a positive impact. Ronald Marx and colleagues (2004) report data on nearly eight thousand middle school students over a span of three years from a science education program that emphasized inquiry-based learning. The results reveal statistically significant increases on curriculum-based test scores for each year of participation. Moreover, the strength of the effects grew over the years. The study indicates that an inquiry-based curriculum could help historically low-achieving science students in an underperforming urban school district succeed in science learning. A later study by the same research team (Geier et al., 2008) indicates that inquiry-based instruction could also reduce the gender gap in achievement experienced by urban African American boys.

Ted Bredderman (1983) conducted a meta-analysis of the impact inquiry-based learning has on students' science achievement. He reports an average effect size of 0.35 when teaching science using inquiry-based methods. The difference is about 13 percentile points. Furthermore, the mean effect on science process (with a mean effect size of 0.52, a difference of 20 percentile points) is much greater than the mean effect on science content (with a mean effect size of 0.28, a difference of 11 percentile points). A 2009 synthesis of meta-analyses by Hattie finds that inquiry-based learning has an effect size of 0.31 (an increase of 12 percentile points).

Research has also focused on the effects of specific instructional programs or initiatives related to inquiry-based learning. For instance, Daniel Hickey, Ann Kindfield, Paul Horwitz, and Mary Ann Christie (1999) find that secondary students who used GenScope, an open-ended software program designed for inquiry-based learning on the subject of genetics, make significantly larger gains than their peers in comparison groups. They also find that students from general science and general biology classrooms make the largest gains when compared with more advanced learners. A quasi-experimental study by Sharon Lynch, Joel Kuipers, Curtis Pyke, and Michael Szesze (2005) examines the impact of inquiry-based curriculum reform on the achievement of eighth-grade students in a culturally diverse Maryland school district. The authors note that all subgroups—based on demographic variables such as ethnicity, socioeconomic status, and gender—in the inquiry-based curriculum group attained higher achievement gains than the comparison group. In addition to academic achievement in science, the findings also indicate that inquiry-based learning positively influences engagement and mastery goal orientation among disadvantaged students.

Researchers also examine the differential impact of different types of inquiry-based methods on science instruction. For instance, Tassanee Bunterm et al. (2014) note the effects of two types of inquiry—guided versus structured inquiry—on secondary students' learning of science. In the structured-inquiry condition, the teachers provide the questions and procedures to students, withholding only the solution; in the guided-inquiry condition, teachers provide only the questions. Bunterm et al. (2014) find that students in the guided-inquiry condition show greater improvement in both science content knowledge and science process skills (see table 8.1).

Table 8.1: Effect Sizes of Inquiry-Based Learning (in Relation to Pretest)

	Guided-Inquiry Condition	Structured-Inquiry Condition
Science content knowledge	0.85 (a gain of 30 percentile points)	0.70 (a gain of 26 percentile points)
Science process skills	0.74 (a gain of 27 percentile points)	0.58 (a gain of 22 percentile points)

Source: Bunterm et al., 2014.

Margaret Blanchard et al. (2010) say that the guided-inquiry approach leads to larger learning gains measured by posttest than traditional verification laboratory instruction (in which teachers direct students to follow explicit, step-by-step laboratory procedures and guide them toward an expected conclusion), especially among students from a high-poverty school. Other studies note that an open-inquiry environment (in which students generate the question, procedures, and solution) is more effective than a structured-inquiry and guided-inquiry approach when teaching high school biology (Sadeh & Zion, 2009, 2012).

Quality inquiry-based learning requires teachers to have robust content knowledge and exploratory skills. Teachers may hesitate to engage in scientific explanations at the elementary level (Löfgren, Schoultz, Hultman, & Björklund, 2013) and face difficulty triggering students' previous knowledge (Kotul'áková, 2013). Teachers also find it challenging to propose a full and reliable inquiry plan, distinguish results from conclusions, and support students with constructive comments (Zion & Mendelovici, 2012). To help teachers avoid this fear and hesitation, the next section details how to incorporate inquiry-based learning for students in the classroom.

How to Move From Research to Practice

Joyce et al. (2004) suggest that the essence of inquiry-based learning is to confront students with genuine problems in an area of investigation. Although teachers do not play as central a role in inquiry learning as in some other instructional strategies, such as direct instruction, scaffolding and facilitating are important. In particular, helping students identify the conceptual or methodological problems within an area of investigation and inviting them to design ways of overcoming those problems are both crucial. Additionally, teachers need to communicate the expectation that students should not only tackle the content but also learn the inquiry process involved in a given situation.

To help teachers, Joyce et al. (2004) propose a five-phase model of inquiry learning.

1. **Confront a puzzling situation:** The teacher presents the problem situation and explains inquiry procedures.

2. **Gather and verify data:** Students gather information about the objects and events based on what they experience and verify the occurrence of the problem situation.

3. **Experiment:** Students isolate relevant variables, hypothesize, and test causal relationships.

4. **Formulate an explanation:** Students organize the data and formulate explanations.

5. **Analyze the inquiry process:** Students determine the most effective questions and the types of information they need but have not acquired, then develop more effective ones for the future.

Judith Lederman (2011) offers another helpful framework—the 5Es Learning Cycle. See table 8.2 for more details.

To put scientific inquiry instruction into practice, the National Research Council (2000) developed the National Science Education Standards, which enumerate skills necessary for students to enact scientific inquiry. Based on the NRC standards, students should be able to do the following.

- Identify and refine questions that guide scientific investigations

- Design and conduct scientific investigations

- Use tools and technology to gather and analyze data

- Formulate and revise findings using evidence and logic

- Recognize and analyze alternative explanations

- Communicate procedures and findings, and defend a scientific argument

Table 8.2: The 5Es Learning Cycle

Engagement	• Present students with unfamiliar phenomena, objects, events, and questions to create need for or interest in learning, and have them make connections with what they already know. • Have students identify problems to solve and consider plans to find answers. • Ascertain prior learning and address misconceptions.
Exploration	• Direct students to actively examine and manipulate objects and phenomena through teacher-organized activities. • With teacher guidance, students share a common base of experience with guidance.
Explanation	• Have students explain their understanding of the concepts and processes they have been exploring. • Prompt students to explain how they know their predictions make sense and to anticipate what they would do differently next time.
Elaboration	• Have students apply concepts and abilities in new contexts to extend understanding and skill. • Allow students to design and carry out their own investigations.
Evaluation	• Direct students to assess their own knowledge, skills, and abilities. • Evaluate student development, lesson effectiveness, and plans for future instructional adjustments.

Inquiry-based learning, then, is a great way to work these standards into everyday classroom instruction.

Another important consideration for using inquiry in classrooms is whether there is a supportive learning environment conducive to inquiry-based instruction. Barbara Crawford, Joseph Krajcik, and Ronald Marx (1999) suggest seven strategies that can encourage inquiry-based learning to flourish.

1. Tasks connected to real-world applications generate more collaborative interactions.
2. Collaborative interactions increase when participants initiate them.
3. Instructional support facilitates group decision making.
4. Participant ownership increases group productivity.
5. Cognitive awareness improves when participants publicly share results.
6. Interactions with outside experts increase participant investment in a project.
7. Teamwork to answer self-generated questions increases participant outcome ownership.

Figure 8.1 is a sample lesson plan for an eighth-grade teacher using inquiry learning. In this lesson, students will use what they've learned about matter and density to predict flotation. The students are beginning to get into density's impact on matter.

Note that when teachers design inquiry-based learning, they can combine features across the models based on what they want to accomplish and how much they want to control. For instance, to encourage students to develop the ability to ask scientifically oriented questions, a teacher can focus on the component of the question and give students opportunities to practice generating questions.

Summary

Inquiry-based learning has the potential to foster deep understanding through hands-on and minds-on learning. It recognizes the complexity in knowledge construction and provides students with opportunities to collaboratively formulate and test their explanations. The key components include identifying problems; designing and executing investigations; making observations; collecting, analyzing, and interpreting data or evidence; supporting claims with evidence; and communicating the findings and explanations. The whole process is facilitated by the teacher, who also can determine how open or how closed the inquiry is by delegating different levels of control to students.

Inquiry is both content and a way to learn and think about the content (used most prominently in science education). The handout "Cycle of Inquiry" (page 74) organizes questions to guide students' thought processes. The teacher can share this chart with students or post it on the wall to provide thinking prompts.

One helpful way to configure inquiry-based learning in a classroom is to use the taxonomy of scientific inquiry, which is based on levels of teacher control or student self-direction: structured inquiry, guided inquiry, and open inquiry (Bell, Smetana, & Binns, 2005; National Research Council, 2000). The handout "Taxonomy of Inquiry" (page 75) depicts how inquiry-based learning can range from highly teacher directed to highly student centered, based on the amount of information teachers provide to the student.

Inquiry-based learning is demanding in terms of teachers' scientific knowledge and skills. Teachers need to have a solid knowledge base and instructional acumen to challenge and support student exploratory learning. We developed the handout "Inquiry-Based Learning Self-Assessment" (page 76) for teachers to self-assess their abilities when engaging students in inquiry-based learning.

Learning Objective(s)

Students will be able to predict whether substances will sink or float by comparing densities.

Procedures

1. Do the "Is It Matter?" activity. Students look at a list of items that are considered matter and items that are not considered matter. They put an *X* next to the items they consider to be matter. Afterward, they describe the rule or reason they used to decide whether something is or is not matter. (This is a quick review of the previous days' lessons on matter.) Call on several students to go to the whiteboard and post their answers. Together, analyze the answers, discuss differences, and clarify students' thinking about matter.

2. Introduce today's lesson. Read a short passage that outlines information about density, floating, and sinking. Tell students this is what they will be learning today. With students, cocreate a T-chart used to predict which objects will float and which will sink. Use the majority of students' predictions for the class-constructed T-chart.

3. Use guided practice. With students, test floating and sinking objects and compare them to student predictions. Students answer your questions about objects and density aloud.

4. Check for understanding. Circulate the room as the students complete their predictions and their questions. This way, you can see and hear who understands and who does not. Question them to ascertain understanding.

5. Use independent practice. Students work to form their conclusions about densities of different objects. Is there a relationship between density and floating and sinking in water? If so, they describe what the relationship is. Circulate as they work. Students share their conclusions.

Closure

Recap the lesson with the students and review the homework assignment.

Assessment

Formative: Use observation and questions to assess student understanding.

Summative: Use a quiz related to the lab work on Friday for the summative assessment. (Students will predict which objects will float or sink, test their hypothesis, and revise their thoughts based on the outcome of their testing. They will explain their conclusions based on what they have learned about properties of matter and density, to include calculating the formula.)

Homework

Students complete questions on page 20 of the text by Thursday.

Figure 8.1: Sample lesson plan.

Cycle of Inquiry

- What do I want to know about this topic?
- What do I know about my question?
- How do I know it?
- What do I need to know?
- What could an answer be?

- What kind of evidence do I need?
- Where do I find it?
- What strategies do I use? Observation, experimentation, or another means of investigation?
- How do I know the evidence is valid?

- What parts do not support my answer?
- Do they raise new questions?
- What are the possible alternative explanations?

Formulating Questions

Collecting Evidence

Developing Explanations

Communicating Results and Justifying Explanations

Testing or Evaluating Explanations

- Who is my audience?
- How do I summarize my evidence and explanations?
- How do I use diagrams or graphs to represent my findings?
- How do I use media to express my message?
- Do I use appropriate scientific terms and communicate with understanding?

- How is this evidence relevant to my question?
- What parts support my answer?
- How does it relate to what else I know?

Taxonomy of Inquiry

Structured Inquiry	Guided Inquiry	Open Inquiry
Students engage in question provided by teacher.	Students sharpen or clarify questions provided by teacher, or select among questions.	Teacher allows students to formulate the question to investigate.
Teacher gives students data and tells them how to analyze them.	Teacher directs students to collect certain data and guides them on data analysis.	Students determine what constitutes evidence and collect it.
Teacher gives explanations from evidence.	Teacher gives students possible ways or guides them to formulate explanations from evidence.	Students formulate explanations based on evidence collected.
Teacher gives students steps and procedures for communicating explanations.	Teacher provides students with guidelines or coaches them on communication of findings.	Students communicate and justify explanations on their own.

Inquiry-Based Learning Self-Assessment

Self-Assessment Statement	Not at All	Very Little	Somewhat	To a Great Extent
I encourage students to support their ideas and opinions with evidence.				
I use open-ended questions that encourage investigation, observation, and thinking.				
I encourage students to ask *how*, *why*, and *what if* questions, rather than just *yes* or *no*, *which*, *who*, *when*, *where*, and *what* questions.				
My classroom is rich with opportunities for students to experience and explore the world.				
I focus and support inquiries while interacting with students.				
I stimulate discourse among students about scientific ideas.				
I challenge students to accept and share responsibility for their own learning.				
I model skills of science inquiry.				

Self-Assessment Statement	Not at All	Very Little	Somewhat	To a Great Extent
I model the curiosity, the openness to new ideas and data, and the skepticism that characterize learning in the given subject area.				
I respect the diversity of the students and allow for a diversity of strategies for learning.				
I encourage students to design and carry out investigations, collaboratively as well as individually, and to identify variables and clarify what counts as data.				
I make sure students do not simply perform the experiments like a prescribed routine but actually understand and explain what they do and what the results mean.				
I allow for a variety of ways for students to demonstrate their learning (such as multiple means of assessment).				
I help students identify patterns within data and generate viable and reliable claims that are supported by evidence.				
I teach students strategies for using argumentation based on evidence and communicating information.				
I carefully listen to students' ideas, comments, and questions.				

Source: Adapted from National Research Council. (1996). National Science Education Standards. Washington, DC: National Academies Press.

Instructional Strategies for Effective Teaching © 2016 Solution Tree Press • solution-tree.com

Visit **go.solution-tree.com/instruction** to download this page.

Chapter 9
Self-Regulated Learning

While it's plausible that there are as many nuanced approaches to teaching as there are teachers, preservice teachers certainly learn common methods that characterize their teaching practices. We've included several of those methods, such as cooperative learning and mastery learning, in this book. In fact, the best teachers have a broad, deep repertoire of instructional practices. On a continuum of these commonly used and well-researched teaching and learning practices, direct instruction would likely occupy one end with self-regulated learning on the other. Both of these can play an important role in effective teaching.

Self-regulated learners are aware of the factors that influence learning and are motivated to take responsibility for their own learning. They also have high efficacy for learning and attribute outcomes to factors that are under their control, such as effort and strategy use (Perry & Drummond, 2002). Additionally, self-regulated learners are active participants in their own learning. They have a repertoire of learning and problem-solving strategies that they apply appropriately and are able to monitor their effectiveness in using these strategies to achieve a goal (Pape, Bell, & Yetkin, 2003). This chapter explores the use of self-regulated learning in an effective teacher's classroom.

What Research Says About Self-Regulated Learning

In a review of research using interview and questionnaire measures of students' self-regulatory strategies, researchers discovered that these strategies correlate significantly with measures of course performance, academic grades, and teachers' ratings of students' proactive efforts to learn in class (Zimmerman, 2008). The research review also indicates that students who are more effective in self-regulation seek help more frequently from peers, teachers, and parents and learn more than students who do not seek help. A meta-analysis of forty-one studies that examine the effect of choice (a key attribute of self-regulated learning) finds that providing choice enhances a number of outcomes—such as intrinsic motivation, effort, task performance, and perceived competence—and the impact is more positive for children as compared to adults (Patall, Cooper, & Robinson, 2008).

Research also finds that student self-regulation strategies are developable and teachable. For instance, in a study by Brenda Tracy, Robert Reid, and Steve Graham (2009), third-grade students learned the following.

- A general strategy for planning and writing stories (such as selecting a topic to write about, organizing possible ideas into a writing plan, and using and upgrading a plan when writing) and a genre-specific strategy (such as learning the necessary elements for the specific genre of storytelling)

- Procedures for regulating the use of these strategies, the writing process, and their writing behaviors, such as goal setting, self-monitoring, and self-speech

- Knowledge about the basic purpose and characteristics of good stories

The students who learned a self-regulated strategy wrote stories that were longer, schematically stronger, and qualitatively better than peers in the comparison group who received traditional writing instruction with a focus on spelling, grammar, and so forth. Effect sizes ranged from 0.35 to 0.71 (see table 9.1, page 80). Furthermore, the students who received self-regulated instruction were able to retain the strategies they learned and transfer them when writing in a similar but untaught genre.

Table 9.1: Effect Sizes of Self-Regulated Learning on Writing

Strategy	Effect Sizes
Schematic structure	0.71
Length of stories	0.55
Quality of writing	0.35

Source: Tracy et al., 2009.

Another meta-analysis of student writing found that explicit instruction of self-regulated writing strategies is especially effective, yielding an average effect size of 1.14 on writing for students in grades 4–12, compared with an average effect size of 0.62 for other approaches (Graham & Perin, 2007). A 2014 study by Heidrun Stoeger, Christine Sontag, and Albert Ziegler also finds that fourth-grade students who receive combined interventions on reading strategies and self-regulated learning performed better in reading comprehension than peers who receive neither or those who learned the reading strategies only. In addition, researchers not only find that self-regulated learning relates to academic achievement and problem-solving success (Pape et al., 2003), but also that it predicts students' perceptions of self-efficacy, such as their judgment of their own learning capabilities (Sadi & Uyar, 2013).

How to Move From Research to Practice

Maurice Gibbons (2002) defines *self-regulated learning* as "any increase in knowledge, skill, accomplishment, or personal development that an individual selects and brings about by his or her own efforts using any method in any circumstances at any time" (p. 2). As suggested earlier, one can visualize teacher-directed (direct instruction) and student-directed (self-regulated) learning on opposing ends of a continuum. Table 9.2 depicts selected distinctions between the two approaches.

Gibbons (2002) also provides a set of essential elements to consider when designing and implementing self-regulated learning opportunities.

- Students should have as much control as possible over the learning experience.
- Skill development should be the focus of student-directed learning.
- Students should challenge themselves to reach for their best possible performances.
- Students should manage themselves and their learning obstacles.
- Self-regulated learning should promote self-motivation and self-assessment.

According to Perry and Drummond (2002), students and the teacher function as a community of learners. The teaching and learning context is positive, supportive, and encouraging. Also, the teacher establishes the context in which students understand the particular significance of the learning. Students respect one another and take responsibility for their learning and behavior, and the teacher fosters positive dispositions toward learning. Students share strategies and resources to cultivate broad acceptance and support for individuals' strengths and challenges.

Students and teachers should also engage in complex, cognitively demanding activities (Perry & Drummond, 2002). Challenging tasks prompt students to make connections and integrate learning processes over multiple learning periods, resulting in learning products of

Table 9.2: Teacher-Directed Learning Versus Student-Directed Learning

In Teacher-Directed Learning, the Teacher:	In Student-Directed Learning, the Teacher:
Decides the goals and the content to be studied	Teaches students to set their own goals and eventually choose what they will study
Presents content to students in lessons	Teaches students the skills and processes involved in setting goals, making plans, and initiating actions
Sets exercise and assignments for study	Negotiates student proposals for learning and acting
Monitors completion and assesses accuracy of student work	Guides students through self-directed monitoring
Tests and grades student performance	Reviews students' assessment of their work

Source: Adapted from Gibbons, 2002, p. 13.

appropriate complexity. These tasks require students to think metacognitively and act strategically.

Increasingly, students take control of learning by making choices. According to Perry and Drummond (2002), "Having choices and opportunities to control the degree of challenge posed by particular tasks increases students' interest in and commitment to tasks" (p. 303). They are more likely to persist when they perceive they have ownership of the learning.

Perry and Drummond (2002) also state that evaluation should be nonthreatening. An effective teacher emphasizes that evaluation is not judgmental and does not occur only when the learning is finished; he or she instead embeds it in ongoing activities. Teachers and students value learning processes as well as products, and teachers encourage students to focus "on personal progress and view errors as opportunities to learn. Students are involved in generating evaluation criteria and, therefore, sense they have control over outcomes," thus developing a sense of agency (Perry & Drummond, 2002, p. 303).

An effective teacher provides instrumental support for students' learning (Perry & Drummond, 2002). The teacher combines "explicit instruction and extensive scaffolding to help students acquire the knowledge and skills they need to complete complex tasks independently and successfully" (Perry & Drummond, 2002, p. 303). The teacher also tailors support to meet the needs of individuals.

Barry Zimmerman (2002) suggests that self-regulation relates to self-reliance and self-discipline, and involves self-awareness, self-motivation, and behavioral skills in learning. He proposes that self-regulation comprises the following skills.

- Setting specific proximal goals
- Adopting appropriate strategies for attaining the goals
- Monitoring performance for signs of progress
- Restructuring physical and social context to better facilitate learning
- Managing time efficiently
- Self-evaluating the quality of learning outcomes
- Attributing the results to factors that are controllable (such as strategy use or efforts) rather than uncontrollable (such as luck or innate ability)

Zimmerman (1998, 2002) divides the process of self-regulated learning into three phases.

1. **Forethought phase:** The processes and beliefs that occur before learning
2. **Performance phase:** The processes that occur during learning
3. **Self-reflection phase:** The processes that occur after learning

See figure 9.1 (page 82) for a breakdown of these phases.

To illustrate what self-regulated learning may look like in real classrooms, consider the following rating scale designed by a teacher to help students self-assess their learning (figure 9.2, page 83).

To solicit more information on students' self-regulation, the teacher also had students write a reflection, such as the following:

I understand the importance of monitoring and regulating my own learning. When I look closely at our performance, I can improve and continue to grow. I find it beneficial to use this checklist regularly when we are learning new skills or knowledge. I understand we not only rate ourselves but also reflect on how we might improve. Even for the areas I think I am "outstanding," I still can improve. We have spent time talking about this and have brainstormed ways to improve. We also work in groups to devise ways to improve. This is the most beneficial process to me. When we rate ourselves and identify improvement steps, the teacher often asks us to set goals for improvement by creating steps to follow. It also gives me a good idea about how I am supposed to gauge understanding and helps me stay on track. The process helps me know there are different ways to learn and learning is about continuously selecting the best way to complete the task.

Regardless of which approach teachers use, self-regulated learners are proactive with their own academic learning. They mobilize self-motivation and metacognitive processes and monitor and adjust their own behaviors. Thus, effective teachers use this instructional method to help students grow and become stakeholders in their own learning.

Forethought		
Task analysis	**Performance**	
• Goal setting (proximal, challenging, but attainable goals) • Strategic planning (selecting appropriate strategies)	Self-control	**Self-Reflection**
	• Imagery (using mental images to organize and remember information) • Self-instruction • Attention focusing • Task strategies	Self-judgment
Self-motivation and beliefs		• Self-evaluation (of goal achievement and learning effectiveness) • Attribution (attributing success or failure to internal or external factors, and to controllable or uncontrollable factors)
• Self-efficacy (having the personal capability to learn) • Outcome expectations (thinking the learning is related and has personal consequences) • Intrinsic interest or value (valuing the learning task for its own merits) • Learning goal orientation (valuing the process of learning for its own merits)	Self-monitoring	Self-reaction
	• Self-recording (such as time use and progress) • Self-experimentation (implementing different strategies and testing their effects on outcomes)	• Self-satisfaction or affect (emotions and attitudes toward self) • Adaptive or defensive (attitudes toward changing ineffective strategies and improving learning)

Source: Adapted from Zimmerman, 1998, 2002.

Figure 9.1: Self-regulated learning.

Summary

There are drastic differences between novice learners and expert learners. Novice learners often depend on external feedback, while experts set personal goals, monitor progress toward the goals, and evaluate and adapt their learning strategies. Self-regulation of learning is not a trait that someone either has or is missing. It is a set of skills that students can develop to tackle the challenges of academic tasks.

Self-regulating learning strategies refer to strategies than enable students to be proactive, initiate self-directive processes, and transform their mental abilities into better academic performance. The handout "Self-Regulating Learning Strategies" (page 84) draws on the table layout from Stephen Pape et al. (2003) but adds specific self-regulating strategies to assist students in reporting and reflecting on self-regulation.

In self-regulated learning, teachers help students take on an increasingly autonomous, self-directed role as they progress. One helpful method to promote student self-regulation is establishing learning contracts (a form of action contract or learning agreement) for students to set challenging yet achievable goals, commit to a path to attain those goals, and self-evaluate results. The handout "Learning Contracts" (page 85) provides two examples of learning contracts. Teachers can adapt and modify these for students of different age groups. Teachers can incorporate as many or as few elements as they wish to best meet students' specific learning needs.

The handout "Student Assessment of Self-Regulated Learning" (page 87) builds on Zimmerman's (2002) three phases of self-regulation and provides a number of items for students to consider as they direct their own learning. Do note that we designed this handout with high school students in mind, so it will require modifications for younger learners.

| Name: _____ |
| Topic/Assignment: _____ |

You are (Check One)	Rating	Description	What Can You Do to Improve? (Be specific.)
	I am out-standing in this subject.	I exhibit excellence in every assignment given to me, going the extra mile on effort and presentation. I study for all of my tests and have obtained impressive scores on them. I am in the top of the class when it comes to this subject.	
	I am pretty darn good.	I try my hardest on all assignments, although sometimes I get less than stellar grades. I study for almost all of the tests and receive a mixture of grades—some great, some not-so-great. Overall, I feel I am pretty strong in this subject but still have room to improve.	
	I am about average.	I could take or leave this subject. When I get an assignment, I do enough to finish it and then I stop. There is rarely any extra effort put into the work I turn in, and when compared to most students in this class, I'm right in the middle. I don't, or rarely, study for tests, and I obtain very average grades on them. There is a lot of room to improve in this subject during the next grading period.	
	I am not doing so well.	I struggle with the concepts and don't turn in all of my work. I have a hard time on the tests, rarely getting a good grade. My work is enough to get a grade, but not a very good one. I don't pay attention in class and sometimes goof off during the time given for this subject.	

Figure 9.2: Assessing myself—rating scale.

Self-Regulating Learning Strategies

	In Class	At Home (including time spent)
Monday		
Tuesday		
Wednesday		
Thursday		
Friday		
Weekend		
Self-Reflection		
What were the strengths?		
What improve-ments are needed?		
Strategies Used		

1. Goal setting
2. Time management (setting time lines)
3. Self-instruction
4. Organizing knowledge
5. Seeking information independently
6. Seeking assistance from peers, teachers, and parents
7. Rehearsing and memorizing

8. Studying notes
9. Keeping records and monitoring
10. Reviewing textbooks
11. Reviewing tests
12. Self-motivation
13. Arranging a supportive learning environment

Others: _____

_____

Source: Adapted from Pape, S. J., Bell, C. V., & Yetkin, I. E. (2003). Developing mathematical thinking and self-regulated learning: A teaching experiment in a seventh-grade mathematics classroom. Educational Studies in Mathematics, 53(3), 179–202.

Learning Contracts

Following are two types of learning contracts.

Contract 1

Name: _____ Date: _____

Subject area: _____

My goal and objectives: _____

What I will do to meet the goal and objectives: _____

Date by which I will meet the goal and objectives: _____

(Student's signature)

_____

(Teacher's signature)

_____

Instructional Strategies for Effective Teaching © 2016 J. H. Stronge • solution-tree.com
Visit **go.solution-tree.com/instruction** to download this page.

Contract 2

Name: _____

Subject area: _____

Date commenced: _____ Target date of completion: _____

Objectives

- What am I going to learn?

Resources and learning strategies

- How am I going to learn?

Outcomes

- What am I going to produce?

Criteria

- How and by whom will my work be assessed?

(Student's signature)

_____

(Teacher's signature)

_____

Instructional Strategies for Effective Teaching © 2016 J. H. Stronge • solution-tree.com
Visit **go.solution-tree.com/instruction** to download this page.

Student Assessment of Self-Regulated Learning

	Not at All	Very Little	Fairly Well	Quite Well	Very Well
Forethought Phase					
I used planning strategies (such as breaking a task into smaller and shorter segments).					
I accurately envisioned the scope of the work (such as understanding the skills or concepts that I need to learn and the quantity of work).					
I developed challenging but attainable learning goals.					
I had an "I can" mentality.					
Performance Phase					
I monitored my strategy use and tested its effectiveness.					
I monitored my progress toward the objective.					
I changed my strategies as needed to improve productivity.					
I took the initiative to search for information and taught myself new knowledge to complete the task.					
I motivated myself to learn (such as using self-reward, doing stimulating activities to increase interest, and using positive self-talk).					
I created a suitable study space (such as cutting down the noise level, turning off distractions).					
I was able to immediately direct my attention back to the task when I was distracted.					

Instructional Strategies for Effective Teaching © 2016 Solution Tree Press • solution-tree.com

Visit **go.solution-tree.com/instruction** to download this page.

	Not at All	Very Little	Fairly Well	Quite Well	Very Well
I used strategies for attention and concentration (such as scheduling more important work to happen during times of greatest concentration, taking notes, and summarizing what I learned to maintain attention).					
I used time-management strategies (such as using a written or picture schedule and checking off progress and setting an alarm for short time segments).					
Self-Reflection Phase					
I evaluated my work against predetermined criteria or standards.					
I attributed success in learning to strategy use and effort.					
I attributed weakness in learning to strategy use and effort.					

Source: Adapted from Zimmerman, B. J. (2002). Becoming a self-regulated learner: An overview. Theory Into Practice, 41(2), 64–70.

Chapter 10
Meaningful Feedback

Verbal interactions, such as questions and answers from teachers to students and back again, represent a significant part of the academic action that takes place in effective classrooms. Feedback and instruction are closely connected; in fact, they are inseparable in the best classrooms. Providing meaningful feedback is one of the crucial instructional tools that help students attain achievement goals (Erturan-Ilker, 2014). Teacher feedback provides information to students about their performance and is an important source of perceived efficacy and competency. Consequently, it influences motivation in learning, students' further pursuit of achievement goals, and their perceptions of the climate of the lesson (Erturan-Ilker, 2014; Senko & Harackiewicz, 2005). The feedback process supports student engagement in learning and enhances the teacher's ability to monitor the learning process. Essentially, it is an ongoing process in which teachers communicate information to students to help them better understand:

- What they are to learn
- What high-quality performance looks like
- What changes are necessary to improve their learning

Feedback influences learning in many ways, including increased effort, motivation, and engagement. Feedback also provides a venue for students to reach a different viewpoint, confirm what is correct or incorrect, find out alternative strategies, realize new directions to pursue, and identify extra information or elaboration when needed (Hattie, 2009). Philip Winne and Deborah Butler (1994) define feedback as capturing these functions and purposes: "Feedback is information with which a learner can confirm, add to, overwrite, tune, or restructure information in memory, whether that information is domain knowledge, meta-cognitive knowledge, beliefs about self and tasks, or cognitive tactics and strategies" (as cited in Hattie, 2009, p. 174). Therefore, teacher feedback is an important source of information regarding student learning, and it serves as an important mechanism for students to reach both cognitive and affective goals.

What Research Says About Feedback

Research indicates that feedback is especially effective when it focuses on developing students' skills, understanding, and mastery, and then treats mistakes as opportunities to learn (Cauley & McMillan, 2010). According to one report, "Effective feedback targets students' specific misconceptions or errors that occur in a content area or a skill set and that provide informative guidance on what they need to do to maximize their performance" (Stronge & Xu, 2012, p. 21). When giving feedback, effective teachers avoid simple *yes* or *no* answers; rather, they provide informative explanations of what students are doing correctly, what they are not doing correctly, and how to fix it (Chappuis & Stiggins, 2002). According to Nugrahenny Zacharias (2007), while teachers report that providing feedback can be "arduous and painstaking," they also feel that it is "an important part of instruction" (as cited in Stronge & Xu, 2012, p. 21).

Hattie's (2009) research synthesis on feedback finds an average effect size of 0.73. This is equivalent to an achievement gain of 27 percentile points. Of course, research also shows that these gains may differ depending on the type of feedback and the way it is given (Hattie & Timperley, 2007). Feedback focusing on task, product, process, and self-regulation is most successful.

In fact, the most effective form of feedback provides cues and reinforcement to the learner and relates to learning goals (Hattie, 2009). However, simply telling students whether their answers are right or wrong has a negative impact on learning, and when the teacher provides the correct answer, the feedback has only a small positive effect (with an average effect size of 0.22) (Marzano, Pickering, & Pollock, 2001).

Robert Marzano, Debra Pickering, and Jane Pollock (2001) find that the most effective feedback involves an explanation of what is accurate and what is inaccurate in student responses, with an average effect size of 0.53. Feedback that encourages students to keep trying until they succeed is effective as well, and also has an average effect size of 0.53. Furthermore, Erturan-Ilker (2014) finds interesting interactions between types of feedback and students' mode of achievement goals, as shown in table 10.1.

In the end, the key to effective feedback is that students receive and act on it (Hattie, 2009).

It's interesting that students as well as teachers have strong beliefs about the importance of feedback. For instance, "students report that informative feedback makes them aware of their mistakes, highlights ways to make corrections, and informs them of teacher expectations" (Stronge, 2013, p. 56). Overall, research (Brookhart, 2008; Hattie & Timperley, 2007; Shute, 2008) shows that when feedback provides explicit guidance, students can adjust their learning in the following ways.

- There is greater impact of achievement.

- Students are more likely to take risks with their learning.

- Students are more likely to keep trying until they succeed.

According to Hattie (2012), students see the value of feedback in a similar way regardless of achievement level. When students have the following perceptions of the feedback they receive, the feedback tends to have the highest relationship to achievement (Hattie, 2012).

- Feedback clarifies my doubts about the task.

- Feedback indicates the quality of my work.

- Feedback helps me elaborate on my ideas.

- Feedback sounds like constructive criticism.

- Feedback sounds like very specific comments.

- Feedback provides work examples that help me think more deeply.

Holistically, Hattie's research indicates that when feedback is able to pinpoint the discrepancy between students' current task performance and the learning intention, it is likely to be most effective. Feedback comes in different forms. Teachers need to be adept in using all of them depending on the type of learning goals to attain.

How to Move From Research to Practice

Effective teachers recognize the importance of feedback on students' work. They "provide feedback in a timely manner and ensure that it relates specifically to the criteria of the task" (Stronge, 2007, p. 89). The amount of time between the activity and the feedback

Table 10.1: Types of Feedback in Relation to Achievement Goals

Types of Achievement Goals	Pekrun, Cusack, Murayama, Elliot, and Thomas (2014)	Cianci, Schaubroeck, and McGill (2010)
Mastery goals (Goals that are self-referential and focus on learning and developing skills)	Self-referential feedback has a positive impact on mastery goals.	Negative feedback has a positive impact on mastery goals.
Performance goals (Goals that are normative in nature and focus on demonstrating competence and outperforming peers)	Normative feedback has a positive impact on performance goals.	Positive feedback has a positive impact on performance goals.

Source: Erturan-Ilker, 2014.

has a critical effect on student achievement (see, for example, Bangert-Drowns, Kulik, Kulik, & Morgan, 1991). In fact, "the longer the delay in giving feedback, the less likely students will respond to the feedback and the less likely learning will be enhanced" (Stronge, 2007, p. 89). So, how soon must *timely* feedback take place? The best answer is to introduce it as early as possible. In some situations, immediate feedback is ideal; in others, teachers need time to evaluate and process student performance before giving feedback. However, the key is sooner rather than later. Remember: the potential for learning is in the feedback far more than in the assignment itself.

It's also important to remember that effective instructional feedback is primarily corrective and informative (Black & Wiliam, 1998; Marzano et al., 2001). Teachers should "avoid simply indicating right or wrong answers, because this practice can actually have a negative impact on student learning. Instead, effective teachers provide specific explanations of what students are doing correctly, what they are not doing correctly, and how to fix it" (Chappuis & Stiggins, 2002, as cited in Stronge, 2007, p. 89). In return, students tend to complete higher-quality work when teachers give them corrective feedback related to the content of the assignment compared to when they receive no corrective feedback (Matsumura, Patthey-Chavez, Valdes, & Garnier, 2002). Hattie (2009) comments that when teachers combine feedback with a correctional review of student learning, it becomes intertwined with instruction. To be effective in its instructional role, then, feedback should provide "information specifically relating to the task or process of learning that fills a gap between what is understood and what is aimed to be understood" (Hattie, 2009, p. 174).

Grant Wiggins (2012) provides seven attributes of effective feedback.

1. **Goal-referenced:** Effective feedback requires a goal and that students are taking actions to achieve it; they should receive goal-related information about their actions.

2. **Tangible and transparent:** Effective feedback should be clear, unambiguous, and indicative of tangible results related to the goal.

3. **Actionable:** Feedback such as "good job" is not actionable. Effective feedback is concrete, specific, and empowering so that students can take further actions.

4. **User-friendly:** Effective feedback is customized and personalized to students' development levels. It focuses on one or two key elements of performance, rather than overloading students with excessive or technical information.

5. **Timely:** Effective feedback allows students the opportunity to use it while their attempts at and the effects of learning are still fresh in their minds.

6. **Ongoing:** Effective feedback is a formative loop—students can start over immediately whenever they fail and continuously get fresh opportunities to receive feedback and learn from it.

7. **Consistent:** Effective feedback provides information that is stable, accurate, and trustworthy—for instance, using highly descriptive rubrics to anchor products and performances.

Wiggins (2012) also recommends that feedback should inform progress toward long-term goals. Effective feedback allows students to adjust their learning pace against a concrete goal or the final performance standards, rather than just providing information on short-term outcomes.

Research shows that most feedback that students obtain in a classroom is from other students, and most of this feedback is incorrect (Hattie, 2009). Therefore, it is essential that students learn how to critically examine their own work and provide constructive and accurate criticism to others (Black, Harrison, Lee, Marshall, & Wiliam, 2004; Black & Wiliam, 1998; Chappuis & Stiggins, 2002; Marzano et al., 2001). In fact, effective teachers take the time to teach students how to provide constructive criticism.

A useful tool for many teachers is a rubric that provides students with the "parameters of success before working on the assignment" (Stronge, 2007, p. 89); students can then assess their own work prior to submitting it to the teacher. Subsequently, the teacher can use the same rubric for feedback and students can use it when critiquing other students' work. Also, depending on the assignment, "offering students an opportunity to incorporate the feedback and resubmit work for additional credit is a worthwhile venture that reinforces the value of revisions" (Stronge, 2007, p. 89). Thus, the effective teacher builds students' capacity to think critically about their own work and the work of others.

Summary

Research generally finds feedback crucial to both motivating learning and improving student knowledge and skill acquisition. Effective teachers take into account the students' current understanding and ability level to provide informative and timely information to their performance on tasks. Feedback can be positive or negative and self-referenced or norm-referenced. It can also be directive, telling students explicitly what needs to be corrected, or facilitative, providing comments to guide students in addressing misconceptions themselves.

The handout "Practice: Critiquing Teacher Feedback" provides a practice activity to critique two teachers' feedback. Teachers should read the student persuasive writing sample and two different teachers' feedback scenarios: one exemplar and one non-exemplar. Teachers can then use the effective feedback criteria as a guide to critique the feedback that each teacher gives to the student, adding comments and suggestions as desired.

Susan Brookhart (2008) presents a very systematic and structured look at the content components of effective feedback. The handout "Analyzing Teacher Feedback" (page 96) builds on her work to provide a framework for teachers and instructional leaders to analyze and improve classroom feedback. The text boxes underneath each component provide guiding recommendations that teachers can use as a reference.

The handout "Teacher Feedback: Self-Assessment" (page 98) draws on research-supported practices for providing feedback (Brookhart, 2008; Hattie, 2009; Marzano et al., 2001). To use this tool most effectively, the teacher identifies and reflects on current feedback practices and rates the current level of performance for each attribute on a scale of 1 to 4: 1, needs significant improvement; 2, needs some attention; 3, satisfactory level of consistency and competence; and 4, high level of consistency and competence.

Practice: Critiquing Teacher Feedback

Directions: Recently our school announced that the vending machines in the cafeteria (juice, snacks, and candy) would be removed. Write an essay that states your opinion on this change. Keep in mind that the purpose of the essay is to state your opinion and convince someone else of your point of view. Also remember what we have been learning about persuasive writing. Be sure to check your work for grammar, spelling, and punctuation.

Henry's Paragraph

Juice is good for you and you should drink it every day. I like orange juice best but my grandma say I should drink cranbury instead. I think she say that because that is the kind of juice she like. So it would be good to have juice machines in the cafeteria.

I don't think its fare that they took our snack machine away because kid's need snacks sometime. We working hard here and we gonna miss the snacks. If they gonna take the snack machine they gotta give us some other thing to eat beside that bad cafeteria food.

Effective Feedback Criteria

Feedback Criteria	Yes or No	Comments (strengths and weaknesses)
Provide feedback that addresses what is correct and elaborates on what students need to do next.		
Provide criterion-referenced feedback.		
Engage students in the feedback process.		
Provide goal-referenced feedback.		
Provide actionable feedback ("good job" is not actionable).		
Provide user-friendly feedback (specific and personalized).		

Teacher Feedback Examples (Seventh Grade)

Teacher A

Miss A: My gosh, Henry! Were you here when we worked on persuasive writing?

Henry: Yep!

Instructional Strategies for Effective Teaching © 2016 J. H. Stronge • solution-tree.com
Visit **go.solution-tree.com/instruction** to download this page.

Miss A: Well, you must have been asleep. Do you remember when we were talking about writing three paragraphs in persuasive writing?

Henry: Yeah, I did do two paragraphs.

Miss A: Henry, are you planning on passing English this year? Because if you are, you need to start getting your act together. I've seen third graders who write better than this!

Henry: I do want to pass.

Miss A: I am starting to think you aren't willing to work hard enough to be a good student! I think you are thinking about what you are going to have for lunch instead of paying attention in class.

Henry: Oh.

Miss A: Let's look at what you did. You did start the sentences with capital letters. At least you got that right. I'm going to mark all the errors so you can fix them.

Henry: OK.

Miss A: It's not that hard, Henry!

Henry: Oh.

Miss A: Do you want to try this again?

Henry: (*Shrugs.*)

Miss A: I'll let you do this again. But I want three paragraphs this time.

Henry: Oh. (*Rolls eyes.*)

Miss A: Try it again, Henry, and let me see if you have been listening to me.

Teacher B

Mr. B: Henry, let's look at your paragraph.

Henry: OK.

Mr. B: Let's read the directions and be sure you know what I wanted you to do. (*Read the directions together.*)

Mr. B: What did I ask you to do?

Henry: Write about my opinion on the snack machines in the cafeteria.

Mr. B: Yes. Did you do that, Henry?

Henry: Kind of. I did say in the second paragraph that it isn't fair that they took the machines away.

Mr. B: Yes, you did. So when I read that, I know your opinion about the snack machines. Good. Tell me why you wrote this first paragraph.

Henry: Because there was a juice machine before and now there isn't, so I thought I should say something about juice.

Mr. B: I can see what you were thinking, but does that really tell me about your opinion on the machines?

Henry: I guess not.

Mr. B: I have an idea. How about if we start with the second paragraph? You have some good ideas here. Let's work on this one paragraph and make it really good.

Henry: OK. I can do that.

Mr. B: You are right. You can do it. There are some other things.

Henry: There are?

Mr. B: Let's look at your second paragraph. Let's see if there are some parts of it that could be better.

Henry: OK.

Mr. B: Do you remember about our chart of words we aren't going to use in our writing? Our "tombstone" words?

Henry: Yeah, we have a chart of those words.

Mr. B: Look at your writing. Did you use any of those words in your second paragraph?

Henry: Yeah, I did. I have *gotta* and *gonna*. Are those bad words?

Mr. B: No, Henry. They are not bad words. They are words we might use when we are talking to someone but we should not use those words in our written work if we want it to be correct. That's why we have the chart. We all say words like *gonna* sometimes, but when we are writing something we should try not to use those words.

Henry: OK.

Mr. B: Henry, let me show you one more item. You also had a problem with contractions. Look at that again. I know you know about contractions. I want you to check with your writing partner before you turn this in to me again.

Henry: OK. I think I can do this.

Mr. B: Henry, I know you can. Now go do it!

Instructional Strategies for Effective Teaching © 2016 J. H. Stronge • solution-tree.com
Visit **go.solution-tree.com/instruction** to download this page.

Analyzing Teacher Feedback

Feedback Content Components	Goal Checklist	Comments: Effective? Yes or No? Rationale
Focus	The feedback focuses: ☐ On the work itself ☐ On the process the student used to do the work ☐ On the student's self-regulation ☐ Not on the student personally	
Recommendations: • When possible, feedback should describe both the work and the process as well as their relationship. • Feedback can comment on the student's self-regulation if the comment will foster self-efficacy. • Avoid personal, noninstructional comments.		
Comparison	The feedback compares student work: ☐ To criteria of exemplary work (criterion-referenced) ☐ To other students (norm-referenced) ☐ To student's own past performance (self-referenced)	
Recommendations: • Use criterion-referenced feedback to give information about the work itself. • Use norm-referenced feedback to give information about learning processes or student effort. • Use self-referenced feedback for students who need to see the progress they are making.		
Function	The feedback is: ☐ Description ☐ Evaluation or judgment	
Recommendations: • Feedback should describe what the teacher observes in the work, such as strengths and weaknesses. • Don't judge in a way that would stop students from trying to improve.		
Valence	The feedback is: ☐ Positive ☐ Negative	

page 1 of 2

Feedback Content Components	Goal Checklist	Comments: Effective? Yes or No? Rationale
Recommendations: • Use positive comments that describe what is well done. • Accompany negative descriptions with positive suggestions for improvement.		
Clarity	The feedback is: ☐ Clear to the student ☐ Unclear to the student	
Recommendations: • Use vocabulary and concepts the student can understand. • Tailor the amount and content of feedback to the student's developmental level. • Check to make sure the student understands the feedback.		
Specificity	The feedback is: ☐ Nitpicky ☐ Just right ☐ Overly general	
Recommendations: • Tailor the degree of specificity to the student and the task. • Make feedback specific enough that students know what to do but not so specific that it's done for them. • Identify errors or types of errors, but avoid correcting every one or supplying right answers.		
Tone	The feedback is: ☐ Responsive ☐ Respectful ☐ Supportive	
Recommendations: • Choose words that communicate respect for the student as a learner. • Choose words that position the student as an agent (active, not passive). • Choose words that inspire the student's thinking, curiosity, or wonder.		

Source: Adapted from Brookhart, S. M. (2008). How to give effective feedback to your students. *Alexandria, VA: Association for Supervision and Curriculum Development.*

Teacher Feedback: Self-Assessment

Scale:

1—Needs significant improvement

2—Needs some attention

3—Satisfactory level of consistency and competence

4—High level of consistency and competence

	On a Scale of 1–4, How Well Are You Achieving Each Component?
I offer three types of feedback appropriately: (1) criterion-referenced feedback (comparing student work to established criteria), (2) norm-referenced feedback (comparing student work to exemplars or other students' work), and (3) self-referenced feedback (comparing student work to his or her own past work).	
I provide feedback that describes strengths and weaknesses, along with strategies for improvement, rather than evaluative or judgmental feedback (such as a summative statement of good or bad quality).	
I provide feedback that describes specific qualities of the work in relation to important learning targets, and the feedback encourages students to be mindful of the learning targets.	
I provide a variety of feedback that focuses on a balanced combination of the student task, product, process, and self-regulation.	
I provide an appropriate combination of positive and negative feedback, and I accompany the negative feedback with constructive suggestions for improvement that do not result in reduced student efficacy in learning.	
I provide feedback that is clear and comprehensible to students, check students' understanding of the feedback, and make sure students act on the feedback.	
I provide feedback that is appropriately specific and provides enough details to be instructive and scaffolded, but not overly detailed, nor does it provide the correct answers directly, so as to deprive students of the opportunity of taking actions and figuring out the problems themselves.	
The tone of my feedback is respectful and supportive, and I am aware of my body language as I communicate.	

Sources: Adapted from Brookhart, S. M. (2008). How to give effective feedback to your students. *Alexandria, VA: Association for Supervision and Curriculum Development; Hattie, J. (2009).* Visible learning: A synthesis of over 800 meta-analyses relating to achievement. *New York: Routledge; Marzano, R. J., Pickering, D. J., & Pollock, J. E. (2001).* Classroom instruction that works: Research-based strategies for increasing student achievement. *Alexandria, VA: Association for Supervision and Curriculum Development.*

Instructional Strategies for Effective Teaching © 2016 Solution Tree Press • solution-tree.com

Visit **go.solution-tree.com/instruction** to download this page.

References and Resources

Afamasaga-Fuata'i, K. (Ed.). (2009). *Concept mapping in mathematics: Research into practice.* New York: Springer.

Algozzine, R., & Maheady, L. (Eds.). (1986). In search of excellence: Instruction that works in special education classrooms. *Exceptional Children, 52,* 487–589.

Alozie, N. M., & Mitchell, C. E. (2014). Getting students talking: Supporting classroom discussion practices in inquiry-based science in real-time teaching. *American Biology Teacher, 76*(8), 501–506.

Al-Shammari, Z., Aqeel, E., Faulkner, P., & Ansari, A. (2012). Enhancing student learning and achievement via a direct instruction–based ICT integrated in a Kuwaiti 12th-grade secondary school math curriculum. *International Journal of Learning, 18*(9), 339–354.

Amiryousefi, M., & Ketabi, S. (2011). Mnemonic instruction: A way to boost vocabulary learning and recall. *Journal of Language Teaching and Research, 2*(1), 178–182.

Baitz, I. (2009). Concept mapping in the online learning environment: A proven learning tool is transformed in a new environment. *International Journal of Learning, 16*(8), 285–292.

Bangert-Drowns, R. L., Kulik, C.-L. C., Kulik, J. A., & Morgan, M. (1991). The instructional effect of feedback in test-like events. *Review of Educational Research, 61*(2), 213–238.

Barton, J. (1995). Conducting effective classroom discussions. *Journal of Reading, 38*(5), 346–350.

Bauer, S. W., & Wise, J. (2009). *The well-trained mind: A guide to classical education at home* (3rd ed.). New York: W. W. Norton.

Baumeister, R. F., & Vohs, K. D. (Eds.). (2004). *Handbook of self-regulation: Research, theory, and applications.* New York: Guilford Press.

Bell, R. L., Smetana, L., & Binns, I. (2005). Simplifying inquiry instruction: Assessing the inquiry level of classroom activities. *The Science Teacher, 72*(7), 30–33.

Benjamin, A. (2003). *Differentiated instruction: A guide for elementary school teachers.* Larchmont, NY: Eye on Education.

Bereiter, C., & Engelmann, S. (1966). *Teaching disadvantaged children in the preschool.* Englewood Cliffs, NJ: Prentice Hall.

Black, P., Harrison, C., Lee, C., Marshall, B., & Wiliam, D. (2004). Working inside the black box: Assessment for learning in the classroom. *Phi Delta Kappan, 86*(1), 9–21.

Black, P., & Wiliam, D. (1998). Assessment and classroom learning. *Assessment in Education: Principles, Policy and Practice, 5*(1), 7–74.

Blanchard, M. R., Southerland, S. A., Osborne, J. W., Sampson, V. D., Annetta, L. A., & Granger, E. M. (2010). Is inquiry possible in light of accountability? A quantitative comparison of the relative effectiveness of guided inquiry and verification laboratory instruction. *Science Education, 94*(4), 577–616.

Block, J. H., & Burns, R. B. (1976). Mastery learning. *Review of Research in Education, 4,* 3–49.

Bloom, B. S. (1984). The 2 sigma problem: The search for methods of group instruction as effective as one-to-one tutoring. *Educational Researcher, 13*(6), 4–16.

Boekaerts, M., Pintrich, P. R., & Zeidner, M. (Eds.). (2000). *Handbook of self-regulation*. San Diego, CA: Academic Press.

Botts, D. C., Losardo, A. S., Tillery, C. Y., & Werts, M. G. (2014). A comparison of activity-based intervention and embedded direct instruction when teaching emergent literacy skills. *Journal of Special Education*, 48(2), 120–134.

Boulware, B. J., & Crow, M. L. (2008). Using the concept attainment strategy to enhance reading comprehension. *The Reading Teacher*, 61(6), 491–495.

Bredderman, T. (1983). Effects of activity-based elementary science on student outcomes: A quantitative synthesis. *Review of Educational Research*, 53(4), 499–518.

Brookfield, S. D., & Preskill, S. (2005). *Discussion as a way of teaching: Tools and techniques for democratic classrooms* (2nd ed.). San Francisco: Jossey-Bass.

Brookhart, S. M. (2008). *How to give effective feedback to your students*. Alexandria, VA: Association for Supervision and Curriculum Development.

Bruner, J. S., Goodnow, J. J., & Austin, G. A. (1956). *A study of thinking*. New York: Wiley.

Bunterm, T., Lee, K., Kong, J. N. L., Srikoon, S., Vangpoomyai, P., Rattanavongsa, J., et al. (2014). Do different levels of inquiry lead to different learning outcomes? A comparison between guided and structured inquiry. *International Journal of Science Education*, 36(12), 1937–1959.

Burchers, S., Jr., Burchers, S., III, & Burchers, B. (2013). *Vocabulary cartoons: SAT word power* (4th ed.). Punta Gorda, FL: New Monic Books.

Cauley, K. M., & McMillan, J. H. (2010). Formative assessment techniques to support student motivation and achievement. *Clearing House: A Journal of Education Strategies, Issues and Ideas*, 83(1), 1–6.

Chang, K.-E., Sung, Y.-T., & Chen, S. F. (2001). Learning through computer-based concept mapping with scaffolding aid. *Journal of Computer Assisted Learning*, 17(1), 21–33.

Chang, K.-E., Sung, Y.-T., & Chen, I.-D. (2002). The effect of concept mapping to enhance text comprehension and summarization. *Journal of Experimental Education*, 71(1), 5–23.

Changeiywo, J. M., Wambugu, P. W., & Wachanga, S. W. (2011). Investigations of students' motivation towards learning secondary school physics through mastery learning approach. *International Journal of Science and Mathematics Education*, 9(6), 1333–1350.

Chappuis, S., & Stiggins, R. J. (2002). Classroom assessment for learning. *Educational Leadership*, 60(1), 40–43.

Cheema, A. B., & Mirza, M. S. (2013). Effect of concept mapping on students' academic achievement. *Journal of Research and Reflections in Education*, 7(2), 125–132.

Chinn, C. A., O'Donnell, A. M., & Jinks, T. S. (2000). The structure of discourse in collaborative learning. *Journal of Experimental Education*, 69(1), 77–97.

Cianci, A. M., Schaubroeck, J. M., & McGill, G. A. (2010). Achievement goals, feedback, and task performance. *Human Performance*, 23(2), 131–154.

Colburn, A. (2000). An inquiry primer. *Science Scope*, 23(6), 42–44.

Crawford, B. A., Krajcik, J. S., & Marx, R. W. (1999). Elements of a community of learners in a middle school science classroom. *Science Education*, 83(6), 701–723.

Darch, C., Gersten, R., & Taylor, R. (1987). Evaluation of Williamsburg County direct instruction program: Factors leading to success in rural elementary programs. *Research in Rural Education*, 4(3), 111–118.

Diegelman-Parente, A. (2011). The use of mastery learning with competency-based grading in an organic chemistry course. *Journal of College Science Teaching*, 40(5), 50–58.

Dunn, M. W. (2011). Writing-skills instruction: Teachers' perspectives about effective practices. *Journal of Reading Education, 37*(1), 18–25.

Durkin, K., & Rittle-Johnson, B. (2012). The effectiveness of using incorrect examples to support learning about decimal magnitude. *Learning and Instruction, 22,* 206–214.

Emmer, E. T., & Gerwels, M. C. (2002). Cooperative learning in elementary classrooms: Teaching practices and lesson characteristics. *Elementary School Journal, 103*(1), 75–91.

Erturan-Ilker, G. (2014). Effects of feedback on achievement goals and perceived motivational climate in physical education. *Issues in Educational Research, 24*(2), 152–161.

Ewens, W. (1986). The organizational behavior teaching review. *Journal of the Organizational Behavior Teaching Society, 10,* 77–80.

Fox, E. J., & Sullivan, H. J. (2007). Comparing strategies for teaching abstract concepts in an online tutorial. *Journal of Educational Computing Research, 37*(3), 307–330.

Gagné, R. M. (1985). *The conditions of learning* (4th ed.). New York: Holt, Rinehart & Winston.

Geier, R., Blumenfeld, P. C., Marx, R. W., Krajcik, J. S., Fishman, B., Soloway, E., et al. (2008). Standardized test outcomes for students engaged in inquiry-based science curricula in the context of urban reform. *Journal of Research in Science Teaching, 45*(8), 922–939.

Gibbons, M. (2002). *The self-directed learning handbook: Challenging adolescent students to excel.* San Francisco: Jossey-Bass.

Gillies, R. M., & Ashman, A. F. (Eds.). (2003). *Co-operative learning: The social and intellectual outcomes of learning in groups.* New York: Routledge.

Gillies, R. M., & Boyle, M. (2010). Teachers' reflections on cooperative learning: Issues of implementation. *Teaching and Teacher Education, 26*(4), 933–940.

Graham, S., & Perin, D. (2007). A meta-analysis of writing instruction for adolescent students. *Journal of Educational Psychology, 99*(3), 445–476.

Grammer, J., Coffman, J. L., & Ornstein, P. (2013). The effect of teachers' memory-relevant language on children's strategy use and knowledge. *Child Development, 84*(6), 1989–2002.

Grant, L., Stronge, J., Xu, X., Popp, P., Sun, Y., & Little, C. (2014). *West meets east: Best practices from expert teachers in the U.S. and China.* Alexandria, VA: Association for Supervision and Curriculum Development.

Guo, S., Tsai, C., Chang, F. M., & Huang, H. (2007). The study of questioning skills on teaching improvement. *International Journal of Learning, 14*(8), 141–145.

Gür, H., & Barak, B. (2007). The erroneous derivative examples of eleventh grade students. *Educational Sciences: Theory and Practice, 7*(1), 473–480.

Guskey, T. R. (2010). Lessons of mastery learning. *Educational Leadership, 68*(2), 52–57.

Guskey, T. R., & Pigott, T. D. (1988). Research on group-based mastery learning programs: A meta-analysis. *Journal of Educational Research, 81*(4), 197–216.

Hale, M. S., & City, E. A. (2006). *The teacher's guide to leading student-centered discussions: Talking about texts in the classroom.* Thousand Oaks, CA: Corwin Press.

Hammerman, E. (2006). *8 essentials of inquiry-based science, K–8.* Thousand Oaks, CA: Corwin Press.

Hattie, J. (2009). *Visible learning: A synthesis of over 800 meta-analyses relating to achievement.* New York: Routledge.

Hattie, J. (2012). *Visible learning for teachers: Maximizing impact on learning.* New York: Routledge.

Hattie, J., & Timperley, H. (2007). The power of feedback. *Review of Educational Research, 77*(1), 81–112.

Heemsoth, T., & Heinze, A. (2014). The impact of incorrect examples on learning fractions: A field experiment with 6th grade students. *Instructional Science, 42*(4), 639–657.

Henning, J. E., McKeny, T., Foley, G. D., & Balong, M. (2012). Mathematics discussions by design: Creating opportunities for purposeful participation. *Journal of Mathematics Teacher Education, 15*(6), 453–479.

Hickey, D. T., Kindfield, A. C. H., Horwitz, P., & Christie, M. A. (1999). Advancing educational theory by enhancing practice in a technology-supported genetics learning environment. *Journal of Education, 181*(2), 25–55.

Holt, L. C., & Kysilka, M. (2006). *Instructional patterns: Strategies for maximizing student learning.* Thousand Oaks, CA: SAGE.

Horton, P. B., McConney, A. A., Gallo, M., Woods, A. L., Senn, G. J., & Hamelin, D. (1993). An investigation of the effectiveness of concept mapping as an instructional tool. *Science Education, 77*(1), 95–111.

Hunter, M. (1976). *Improved instruction.* El Segundo, CA: Theory into Practice.

Hunter, M. (1982). *Mastery teaching.* El Segundo, CA: Theory into Practice.

Hyman, R. T. (1980). *Improving discussion leadership.* New York: Teachers College Press.

Johnson, D. W., & Johnson, R. T. (1989). *Cooperation and competition: Theory and research.* Edina, MN: Interaction Books.

Johnson, D. W., & Johnson, R. T. (1999a). *Learning together and alone: Cooperative, competitive, and individualistic learning* (5th ed.). Boston: Allyn & Bacon.

Johnson, D. W., & Johnson, R. T. (1999b). Making cooperative learning work. *Theory Into Practice, 38*(2), 67–73.

Johnson, D. W., Johnson, R. T., & Roseth, C. (2010). Cooperative learning in middle schools: Interrelationship of relationships and achievement. *Middle Grades Research Journal, 5*(1), 1–18.

Joyce, B., Weil, M., & Calhoun, E. (2004). *Models of teaching* (7th ed.). Boston: Allyn & Bacon.

Kame'enui, E. J., Simmons, D. C., Chard, D., & Dickson, S. (1997). Direct-instruction reading. In S. A. Stahl & D. Hayes (Eds.), *Instructional models in reading* (pp. 59–84). Mahwah, NJ: Erlbaum.

Karpicke, J. D., & Blunt, J. R. (2011). Retrieval practice produces more learning than elaborative studying with concept mapping. *Science, 331*(6018), 772–775.

Khan, S. A., & Ahmad, R. N. (2014). Evaluation of the effectiveness of cooperative learning method versus traditional learning method on the reading comprehension of the students. *Journal of Research and Reflections in Education, 8*(1), 55–64.

Khoii, R., & Sharififar, S. (2013). Memorization versus semantic mapping in L2 vocabulary acquisition. *English Language Teaching Journal, 67*(2), 199–209.

Kotul'áková, K. (2013). Teachers' focus on pupil's prior conceptions in inquiry-based teaching. *Review of Science, Mathematics and ICT Education, 7*(2), 53–71.

Kroesbergen, E. H., Van Luit, J. E. H., & Maas, C. J. M. (2004). Effectiveness of explicit and constructivist mathematics instruction for low-achieving students in the Netherlands. *Elementary School Journal, 104*(3), 233–251.

Ku, K. Y. L., Ho, I. T., Hau, K.-T., & Lai, E. C. M. (2014). Integrating direct and inquiry-based instruction in the teaching of critical thinking: An intervention study. *Instructional Science, 42*(2), 251–269.

Kumar, A., & Mathur, M. (2013). Effect of concept attainment model on acquisition of physics concepts. *Universal Journal of Educational Research, 1*(3), 165–169.

Kyndt, E., Raes, E., Lismont, B., Timmers, F., Cascallar, E., & Dochy, F. (2013). A meta-analysis of the effects of face-to-face cooperative learning: Do recent studies falsify or verify earlier findings? *Educational Research Review, 10*, 133–149.

Lan, W. Y., & Repman, J. (1995). The effects of social learning context and modeling on persistence and dynamism in academic activities. *Journal of Experimental Education, 64*(1), 53–67.

Lederman, J. S. (2011). *Levels of inquiry and the 5 E's Learning Cycle model.* Monterey, CA: National Geographic School.

Ledford, J. R., Lane, J. D., Elam, K. L., & Wolery, M. (2012). Using response-prompting procedures during small-group direct instruction: Outcomes and procedural variations. *American Journal on Intellectual and Developmental Disabilities, 117*(5), 413–434.

LePage, P., Darling-Hammond, L., & Akar, H. (2005). Classroom management. In L. Darling-Hammond & J. Bransford (Eds.), *Preparing teachers for a changing world: What teachers should learn and be able to do* (pp. 327–357). San Francisco: Jossey-Bass.

Löfgren, R., Schoultz, J., Hultman, G., & Björklund, L. (2013). Exploratory talk in science education: Inquiry-based learning and communicative approach in primary school. *Journal of Baltic Science Education, 12*(4), 482–496.

Lynch, S., Kuipers, J., Pyke, C., & Szesze, M. (2005). Examining the effects of a highly rated science curriculum unit on diverse students: Results from a planning grant. *Journal of Research in Science Teaching, 42*(8), 912–946.

Magliaro, S. G., Lockee, B. B., & Burton, J. K. (2005). Direct instruction revisited: A key model for instructional technology. *Educational Technology Research and Development, 53*(4), 41–55.

Martorella, P. (1999). Concept learning and higher-level thinking. In J. M. Cooper (Ed.), *Classroom teaching skills* (6th ed., pp. 155–176). Boston: Houghton Mifflin.

Marx, R. W., Blumenfeld, P. C., Krajcik, J. S., Fishman, B., Soloway, E., Geier, R., et al. (2004). Inquiry-based science in the middle grades: Assessment of learning in urban systemic reform. *Journal of Research in Science Teaching, 41*(10), 1063–1080.

Marzano, R. J., Pickering, D. J., & Pollock, J. E. (2001). *Classroom instruction that works: Research-based strategies for increasing student achievement.* Alexandria, VA: Association for Supervision and Curriculum Development.

Matsumura, L. C., Patthey-Chavez, G. G., Valdes, R., & Garnier, H. (2002). Teacher feedback, writing assignment quality, and third-grade students' revision in lower- and higher-achieving urban schools. *Elementary School Journal, 103*(1), 3–25.

Minner, D. D., Levy, A. J., & Century, J. (2010). Inquiry-based science instruction—What is it and does it matter? Results from a research synthesis years 1984 to 2002. *Journal of Research in Science Teaching, 47*(4), 474–496.

Mnemonic Devices Memory Tools. (n.d.). *What is a mnemonic device?* Accessed at www.mnemonic-device.com /what-is-a-mnemonic-device on February 18, 2015.

Mulryan, C. M. (1992). Student passivity during cooperative small groups in mathematics. *Journal of Educational Research, 85*(5), 261–273.

Mulryan, C. M. (1995). Fifth and sixth graders' involvement and participation in cooperative small groups in mathematics. *Elementary School Journal, 95*(4), 297–310.

Murphy, P. K., Wilkinson, I. A. G., Soter, A. O., Hennessey, M. N., & Alexander, J. F. (2009). Examining the effects of classroom discussion on students' comprehension of text: A meta-analysis. *Journal of Educational Psychology, 101*(3), 740–764.

National Research Council. (1996). *National Science Education Sandards.* Washington, DC: National Academies Press.

National Research Council. (2000). *Inquiry and the National Science Education Standards: A guide for teaching and learning.* Washington, DC: National Academies Press.

Nesbit, J. C., & Adesope, O. O. (2006). Learning with concept and knowledge maps: A meta-analysis. *Review of Educational Research, 76*(3), 413–448.

Novak, J. D., & Cañas, A. J. (2008). *The theory underlying concept maps and how to construct and use them* (Tech. Rep. IHMC CmapTools). Pensacola, FL: Florida Institute for Human and Machine Cognition. Accessed at http://cmap.ihmc.us/Publications/ResearchPapers/TheoryUnderlyingConceptMaps.pdf on February 17, 2015.

Oliver, K. (2009). An investigation of concept mapping to improve the reading comprehension of science texts. *Journal of Science Education and Technology, 18*(5), 402–414.

Orlich, D. C., Harder, R. J., Callahan, R. C., & Gibson, H. W. (2001). *Teaching strategies: A guide to better instruction* (6th ed.). Boston: Houghton Mifflin.

Pape, S. J., Bell, C. V., & Yetkin, I. E. (2003). Developing mathematical thinking and self-regulated learning: A teaching experiment in a seventh-grade mathematics classroom. *Educational Studies in Mathematics, 53*(3), 179–202.

Park, O.-C. (1984). Example comparison strategy versus attribute identification strategy in concept learning. *American Educational Research Journal, 21*(1), 145–162.

Patall, E. A., Cooper, H., & Robinson, J. C. (2008). The effects of choice on intrinsic motivation and related outcomes: A meta-analysis of research findings. *Psychological Bulletin, 134*(2), 270–300.

Pekrun, R., Cusack, A., Murayama, K., Elliot, A. J., & Thomas, K. (2014). The power of anticipated feedback: Effects on students' achievement goals and achievement emotions. *Learning and Instruction, 29*, 115–124.

Perry, N., & Drummond, L. (2002). Helping young students become self-regulated researchers and writers. *The Reading Teacher, 56*(3), 298–310.

Peters, E. E., & Levin, J. R. (1986). Effects of a mnemonic imagery strategy on good and poor readers' prose recall. *Reading Research Quarterly, 21*(2), 179–192.

Plotnick, E. (1997). *Concept mapping: A graphical system for understanding the relationship between concepts.* Syracuse, NY: ERIC Clearinghouse on Information and Technology. (ERIC Digest No. ED407938) Accessed at www.ericdigests.org/1998-1/concept.htm on September 19, 2014.

Prater, M. A. (1993). Teaching concepts: Procedures for the design and delivery of instruction. *Remedial and Special Education, 14*(5), 51–62.

Preast, S. D. (2009). *A study of direct instructional spelling strategies and their effect on students with special needs who are classified with mild mental disabilities.* Unpublished doctoral dissertation, Walden University, Minneapolis, Minnesota.

Pritchard, F. F. (1994). *Teaching thinking across the curriculum with the concept attainment model.* Salisbury, MD: Salisbury University. (ERIC Document Reproduction Service No. ED379303)

Reinsvold, L. A., & Cochran, K. F. (2012). Power dynamics and questioning in elementary science classrooms. *Journal of Science Teacher Education, 23*(7), 745–768.

Reznitskaya, A., Anderson, R. C., McNurlen, B., Nguyen-Jahiel, K., Archodidou, A., & Kim, S.-Y. (2001). Influence of oral discussion on written argument. *Discourse Processes, 32*(2/3), 155–175.

Roberts, D. S., Ingram, R. R., Flack, S. A., & Hayes, R. J. (2013). Implementation of mastery learning in nursing education. *Journal of Nursing Education, 52*(4), 234–237.

Rosenshine, B. (1985). Direct instruction. In T. Husen & T. N. Postlethwaite (Eds.), *International encyclopedia of education* (pp. 1395–1400). Oxford, England: Pergamon Press.

Ross, J. A. (1995). Effects of feedback on student behavior in cooperative learning groups in a grade 7 math class. *Elementary School Journal, 96*(2), 125–143.

Sadeh, I., & Zion, M. (2009). The development of dynamic inquiry performances within an open inquiry setting: A comparison to guided inquiry setting. *Journal of Research in Science Teaching, 46*(10), 1137–1160.

Sadeh, I., & Zion, M. (2012). Which type of inquiry project do high school biology students prefer: Open or guided? *Research in Science Education, 42*(5), 831–848.

Sadi, O., & Uyar, M. (2013). The relationship between self-efficacy, self-regulated learning strategies and achievement: A path model. *Journal of Baltic Science Education, 12*(1), 21–33.

Savery, J. R. (2006). Overview of problem-based learning: Definitions and distinctions. *Interdisciplinary Journal of Problem-Based Learning, 1*(1), 9–20.

Schalock, H. D., Schalock, M. D., Cowart, B., & Myton, D. (1993). Extending teacher assessment beyond knowledge and skills: An emerging focus on teacher accomplishments. *Journal of Personnel Evaluation in Education, 7*, 105–133.

Scruggs, T. E., & Mastropieri, M. A. (1990). Mnemonic instruction for students with learning disabilities: What it is and what it does. *Learning Disability Quarterly, 13*(4), 271–280.

Scruggs, T. E., & Mastropieri, M. A. (1991). Classroom applications of mnemonic instruction: Acquisition, maintenance, and generalization. *Exceptional Children, 58*(3), 219–229.

Scruggs, T. E., & Mastropieri, M. A. (2000). The effectiveness of mnemonic instruction for students with learning and behavior problems: An update and research synthesis. *Journal of Behavioral Education, 10*(2/3), 163–173.

Senko, C., & Harackiewicz, J. M. (2005). Regulation of achievement goals: The role of competence feedback. *Journal of Educational Psychology, 97*(3), 320–336.

Sharan, Y., & Sharan, S. (1992). *Expanding cooperative learning through group investigation.* New York: Teachers College Press.

Shute, V. J. (2008). Focus on formative feedback. *Review of Educational Research, 78*(1), 153–189.

Slavin, R. E. (1991). Synthesis of research of cooperative learning. *Educational Leadership, 48*(5), 71–82.

Slavin, R. E. (1995). *Cooperative learning: Theory, research, and practice* (2nd ed.). Needham Heights, MA: Allyn & Bacon.

Slavin, R. E. (1996). *Education for all: Contexts of learning.* London: CRC Press.

Sousa, D. A. (2011). *How the brain learns* (4th ed.). Thousand Oaks, CA: Corwin Press.

Stevens, R. J., & Slavin, R. E. (1995a). The cooperative elementary school: Effects on students' achievement, attitudes, and social relations. *American Educational Research Journal, 32*(2), 321–351.

Stevens, R. J., & Slavin, R. E. (1995b). Effects of a cooperative learning approach in reading and writing on academically handicapped and nonhandicapped students. *Elementary School Journal, 95*(3), 241–262.

Stevens, R. J., Slavin, R. E., & Farnish, A. M. (1991). The effects of cooperative learning and direct instruction in reading comprehension strategies on main idea identification. *Journal of Educational Psychology, 83*(1), 8–16.

Stoeger, H., Sontag, C., & Ziegler, A. (2014). Impact of a teacher-led intervention on preference for self-regulated learning, finding main ideas in expository texts, and reading comprehension. *Journal of Educational Psychology, 106*(3), 799–814.

Stronge, J. H. (2007). *Qualities of effective teachers* (2nd ed.). Alexandria, VA: Association for Supervision and Curriculum Development.

Stronge, J. H. (2013). *Evaluating what good teachers do: Eight research-based standards for assessing teacher excellence.* New York: Routledge.

Stronge, J. H., Grant, L., & Xu, X. (2015). Teachers and teaching. In J. D. Wright (Ed.), *International encyclopedia of the social and behavioral sciences* (2nd ed., pp. 44–50). Maryland Heights, MO: Elsevier.

Stronge, J. H., & Xu, X. (2012). *Research synthesis of CESA 6 teacher evaluation standards.* Oshkosh, WI: Cooperative Educational Services Agency 6.

Stronge, J. H., Ward, T. J., Tucker, P. D., & Hindman, J. L. (2007). What is the relationship between teacher quality and student achievement? An exploratory study. *Journal of Personnel Evaluation in Education, 20*, 165–184.

Tan, S. C. (2000). The effects of incorporating concept mapping into computer assisted instruction. *Journal of Educational Computing Research, 23*(2), 113–131.

Tennyson, R. D., & Cocchiarella, M. J. (1986). An empirically based instructional design theory for teaching concepts. *Review of Educational Research, 56*(1), 40–71.

Thorne, G. (2006, May 1). *10 strategies to enhance students' memory.* Accessed at www.cdl.org/articles/10-strategies -to-enhance-students-memory on October 10, 2014.

Tracy, B., Reid, R., & Graham, S. (2009). Teaching young students strategies for planning and drafting stories: The impact of self-regulated strategy development. *Journal of Educational Research, 102*(5), 323–332.

Upadhyay, B., & DeFranco, C. (2008). Elementary students' retention of environmental science knowledge: Connected science instruction versus direct instruction. *Journal of Elementary Science Education, 20*(2), 23–37.

van Boxtel, C., van der Linden, J., & Kanselaar, G. (2000). Collaborative learning tasks and the elaboration of conceptual knowledge. *Learning and Instruction, 10*(4), 311–330.

van Boxtel, C., van der Linden, J., Roelofs, E., & Erkens, G. (2002). Collaborative concept mapping: Provoking and supporting meaningful discourse. *Theory Into Practice, 41*(1), 40–46.

van Drie, J., & Dekker, R. (2013). Theoretical triangulation as an approach for revealing the complexity of a classroom discussion. *British Educational Research Journal, 39*(2), 338–360.

Wiggins, G. (2012). Seven keys to effective feedback. *Educational Leadership, 70*(1), 10–16.

Winne, P. H., & Butler, D. L. (1994). Student cognition in learning from teaching. In T. Husen & T. N. Postlethwaite (Eds.), *International encyclopedia of education* (2nd ed., pp. 5738–5745). Oxford, England: Pergamon Press.

Worsley, A. F. (1975). Improving classroom discussions: Ten principles. *Improving College and University Teaching, 23*, 27–28.

Zacharias, N. T. (2007). Teacher and student attitudes toward teacher feedback. *RELC Journal: A Journal of Language Teaching and Research, 38*(1), 38–52.

Zakaria, E., Chin, L. C., & Daud, M. Y. (2010). The effects of cooperative learning on students' mathematics achievement and attitude towards mathematics. *Journal of Social Sciences, 6*(2), 272–275.

Zimmerman, B. J. (1998). Academic studying and the development of personal skill: A self-regulatory perspective. *Educational Psychologist, 33*(2/3), 73–86.

Zimmerman, B. J. (2002). Becoming a self-regulated learner: An overview. *Theory Into Practice, 41*(2), 64–70.

Zimmerman, B. J. (2008). Investigating self-regulation and motivation: Historical background, methodological developments, and future prospects. *American Educational Research Journal, 45*(1), 166–183.

Zion, M., & Mendelovici, R. (2012). Moving from structured to open inquiry: Challenges and limits. *Science Education International, 23*(4), 383–399.

Index

Unstoppable Learning
Douglas Fisher and Nancy Frey

Discover how systems thinking can enhance teaching and learning schoolwide. Examine how to use systems thinking—which involves distinguishing patterns and considering short- and long-term consequences—to better understand the big picture of education and the intricate relationships that impact classrooms. Identify strategies and tools to create clear learning targets, prepare effective lessons, and successfully assess instruction.
BKF662

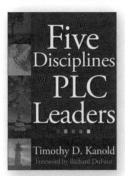

The Five Disciplines of PLC Leaders
Timothy D. Kanold

Outstanding leadership in a professional learning community requires practice and patience. Simply trying harder will not yield results; leaders must proactively train to get better at the skills that matter. This book offers a framework to focus time, energy, and effort on five key disciplines. Included are reflection exercises to help readers find their own path toward effective PLC leadership.
BKF495

On Excellence in Teaching
Edited by Robert J. Marzano

Learn from the world's best education researchers, theorists, and staff developers as they present recommendations on effective instruction. The book provides a comprehensive view of instruction from a theoretical, systemic, and classroom perspective. The authors' diverse expertise delivers a wide range of ideas and strategies.
BKF278

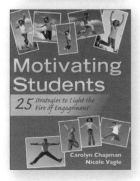

Motivating Students
Carolyn Chapman and Nicole Dimich Vagle

Learn why students disengage and how to motivate them to achieve success with a five-step framework. Research-based strategies and fun activities show how to instill a lasting love of learning in students of any age. Classroom tips and troubleshooting advice for common motivation problems prepare readers for the real-world ups and downs of motivating students.
BKF371

Classroom Habitudes
Angela Maiers

You know students need to acquire 21st century skills. But how do you work those skills into the curriculum? Learn how to use the content you already teach to challenge students to think critically, collaborate with others, solve new problems, and adapt to change across new learning contexts. Help students build the seven habitudes—habits of disciplined decisions and specific attitudes—they need to succeed.
BKF542